Kitchen Witchcraft: Garden Magic

Kitchen Witchcraft: Garden Magic

Rachel Patterson

Winchester, UK
Washington, USA

First published by Moon Books, 2018
Moon Books is an imprint of John Hunt Publishing Ltd., No. 3 East Street, Alresford
Hampshire SO24 9EE, UK
office1@jhpbooks.net
www.johnhuntpublishing.com
www.moon-books.net

For distributor details and how to order please visit the 'Ordering' section on our website.

Text copyright: Rachel Patterson 2017

ISBN: 978 1 78535 766 4
978 1 78535 767 1 (ebook)
Library of Congress Control Number: 2018932657

A CIP catalogue record for this book is available from the British Library.

Design: Stuart Davies

UK: Printed and bound by CPI Group (UK) Ltd, Croydon, CR0 4YY
US: Printed and bound by Thomson-Shore, 7300 West Joy Road, Dexter, MI 48130

We operate a distinctive and ethical publishing philosophy in
all areas of our business, from our global network of authors to
production and worldwide distribution.

Contents

Also by Rachel Patterson

Pagan Portals: Kitchen Witchcraft
Grimoire of a Kitchen Witch
Pagan Portals: Hoodoo Folk Magic
Pagan Portals: Moon Magic
A Kitchen Witch's World of Magical Plants & Herbs
A Kitchen Witch's World of Magical Foods
Pagan Portals: Meditation
The Art of Ritual
Arc of the Goddess (co-written with Tracey Roberts)
Pagan Portals: The Cailleach
Moon Books Gods & Goddesses Colouring Book (Patterson family)
Pagan Portals: Animal Magic
Witchcraft ... into the Wilds
Kitchen Witchcraft Series: Spells & Charms

Who am I?

I am a witch ... have been for a very long time. I am also a working wife and mother who has also been lucky enough to write and have published a book or thirteen. I love to learn, I love to study and have done so from books, online resources, schools and wonderful mentors over the years and continue to learn every day but have learnt the most from getting outside and doing it.

I like to laugh, bake and eat cake ...

I am High Priestess of the Kitchen Witch Coven and an Elder at the online Kitchen Witch School.

I also have regular blogs on:

Witches & Pagans - www.witchesandpagans.com/pagan-paths-blogs/hedge-witch.html

Patheos Pagan - www.patheos.com/blogs/beneaththemoon

Moon Books – www.moon-books.net/blogs/moonbooks/author/rachelp

My website and personal blog: www.rachelpatterson.co.uk

Facebook: www.facebook.com/rachelpattersonbooks

Email: kitchenwitchhearth@yahoo.com

www.kitchenwitchhearth.net

www.kitchenwitchuk.blogspot.co.uk

www.facebook.com/kitchenwitchuk

My craft is a combination of old religion Witchcraft, Kitchen Witchery, Hedge Witchery and folk magic. My heart is that of a Kitchen Witch.

Warning

If you are handling herbs, plants, flowers and essential oils please be aware of any allergies.

Check that you have identified the plants correctly.

With essential oils especially (and some plants) check allergies and toxicity. Some plants are extremely toxic. Some undiluted oils can cause nasty reactions when they come in contact with skin.

Pregnant ladies, elderly and young children should be extremely careful when handling essential oils – check with a qualified practitioner before using.

Welcome to my garden ...

This is not a detailed 'how to' garden book, there are plenty of decent books on the market that will help you decide what to plant, how to look after it and how to garden successfully. Although I do give some hints and tips. The main purpose of this book is to help introduce magic into your outside space.

Whether you only have a window sill with a pot plant on, a small city terrace, a playing field or several acres, you can always work with the magic of your garden. I think the kitchen extends into the garden anyway, so a Kitchen Witch will often be found pottering around in amongst the plants.

Being in regular contact with your garden and what you grow, even with your house plants or a few pots of herbs, can help you to connect with the spirit of nature and recognise the subtleties of the changing of the seasons, and your garden can also provide you with food and magical ingredients.

Magical gardening does take time, focus and attention. You can't just plant something and leave it in the hope that several months later it will have grown, flourished and be covered in fruit or flowers (Okay, on the odd occasion it does happen but not often!).

My gardening memories date back to my childhood. My dad is and always was a keen gardener, organic before it was fashionable to be so. He has always had an allotment and a greenhouse which provide a bounty of wonderful fruit and vegetables. Apparently even as a toddler I would disappear down the garden with him and come back covered in mud.

In my early teens I experienced food production on a large scale as I lived on a farm for a few years. Then in my late teens I had the opportunity of working for a specialist glasshouse company. Both of those life events added to my love of the garden, food and nature's bounty.

3

Once I owned my own house, the garden became key. It is my sanctuary, a peaceful place to escape to and a space in which to create magic.

For the past twenty or so years we have lived in the same house; it is on the edge of a large city and only has a small walled garden, but it is ours and we have packed it full of as many plants, flowers and herbs as we can cram into it. We even have a very small (i.e. teeny tiny) grow house just big enough to overwinter a few pots and grow some seeds.

Even on my busy days I try to step out into the garden, if only just for a few minutes to relax and connect with Mother Earth.

Your garden, whatever size it is, opens up a whole new world of magic for you to delve in to. Warning: Gardening is addictive and will improve your health, spirit and mental well-being.

Not only is a garden your direct line to a natural source of energy, it can also provide you with a whole shopping trolley full of free magical and often edible ingredients; whether it is in the form of fruit and vegetables or flowers, petals and seeds.

Let's open the magical box

You may imagine you need to have a beautiful picture box garden laid out in front of a thatched cottage to have a witch's garden but really that isn't the case. You can style the garden in any way that suits your taste, size of garden and your budget.

Many hours and much money can be spent in garden centres and whilst they are brilliant sources for plant and design inspiration you can spend more money than you need to. Oh ... and a lot of them have a café ... with cake.

Plant nurseries often tend to be cheaper than garden centres but ask around. Lots of family and friends will probably be willing to share cuttings and seeds with you. And once your garden has a few plants in you can propagate more from those you already have.

Gardening does take time and effort. You will need to dig, plant, weed, dead head, water and keep things generally tidy. Even a small garden can eat up the time, but it will be worth the effort. Just bear the time factor in mind when designing your garden and choosing your plants.

Watching something grow and flourish under your care is incredibly rewarding. Add to that, once you establish plants in your garden the wildlife will follow.

Our garden this past summer had so many bees flitting about it was deafening. In fact, I think we got in their way; they seemed incredibly annoyed if we were trying to tend to a plant they were interested in. Along with all the butterflies, birds and of course the wide variety of insects, you may even find other creatures such as toads and hedgehogs begin to visit.

Gardens have gone through many changes over the years and come in many shapes, sizes and varieties: immaculate green lawns with flower borders, back gardens turned over to vegetable plots during the war, concreted over with large patios or decking and all other designs in between.

The plants within though, have long been used for medicinal and magical use.

I think it is worth doing some historical research on garden design before you plan yours out. History can provide inspiration and insight.

Garden magic covers not only plants, trees and flowers but also the use of pebbles, shells, stones and any other manner of natural items to work magic with; including those incredibly annoying spider webs that have a habit of colliding with your face when you walk outside. (Spider webs are very useful ingredients in witch bottles.)

I will talk about the magical properties of flowers, seeds, plants and trees (more detailed information can be found in my other books: *A Kitchen Witch's World of Magical Plants & Herbs* and *A Kitchen Witch's World of Magical Food*) but I also love to work with colour magic, so I will share my thoughts on that too.

Don't think you have to limit your garden to just herbs or fill it with ancient or deadly plants. Each and every type of plant contains magic of some kind, even the humble blade of grass and the wayward weed.

A weed is just a plant growing in the wrong place ...

In the beginning

You may already have a garden in place or at least the basics or you may be starting from scratch. Your first plan of action is to assess it. What type of soil do you have? This will affect the sort of plants you can grow in the ground. What direction does it face, and do you have shady or sunny spots? Plants have requirements, not everything likes full sun and not everything will survive under the shade of a tree or in a windy spot. Take a look around and work out what spaces you have and what conditions they provide for your plants.

What temperature zone do you live in? Some plants won't like the cold and some won't survive if a frost hits. What is your average rainfall? Not all plants like soggy feet. If you get stuck your local nursery/garden centre will be able to advise you.

What access do you need to your garden? Don't block the gates or pathways with flower beds.

What views do you have? Don't block out pretty landscapes, borrow them. If your neighbour has tall trees or hedges use these as a frame or backdrop for your garden. However, if your garden backs onto a commercial warehouse or ugly building you might want to think about plants that will grow upwards to hide it.

Think about how much time you have to tend to the garden. If your time is limited, you may not want to fill it with annuals or vegetables that need a lot of attention. Perennials and shrubs would be better for you.

Don't forget to check the height and spread that a plant is supposed to grow to. And don't always trust the information. We planted a photinia shrub many years ago. The details said it would only grow to a maximum of 6 feet. We didn't prune it much and eventually it reached the height of about 25 feet.

If you want space to sit in the garden, work in room for chairs and even a small table.

Be careful when digging, you don't want to hit gas or water pipes with your shovel.

If you have the space, you may also want to work in room for a small ritual circle or fire pit. Even a small garden may have a little room for an outdoor altar or shrine.

Plan it all out on paper first, cut out clippings from magazines of plants or designs that you like and research for ideas on the internet or in the library. Visit local open gardens, even large stately home gardens can be an inspiration for the smaller garden.

Compost

If you have the room for a compost bin it is worthwhile. We have one the size of a trash can/dustbin and all the vegetable peelings, egg shells and old newspapers get chucked in. There is a whole complicated science around compost and ideally in a large garden you would have two or three compost heaps that you rotate, turn and move regularly. In reality most of us only have room for a single small one, but it still works effectively it just takes a bit longer.

Flow of magic in a garden space

When I was talking about this book one of my lovely friends suggested I write about the 'flow of magic in a garden space', so I will. Have you been in some gardens that immediately feel magical? Or a garden that makes you feel relaxed and peaceful as soon as you step through the gate? That is when the flow of magic has been created perfectly. Occasionally it happens by accident but usually it is the result of lots of careful planning and hard work.

The style of your garden will reflect you and your personality and will probably evolve and change over time. Getting the balance in a garden can be tricky and often involves moving things around until if feels right.

Think about the atmosphere you want in your garden. If you would like it to be peaceful then you may want to keep to a colour palette of cool blues, whites and pinks. A big ole orange flower bed in your face doesn't perhaps convey calm and serenity. But bright colours might suit you better; trust your intuition and what works for you.

Design will also be a key factor. Even in my own small garden we still try to create some 'secret' areas and paths that invite you to walk down them. I like a garden to draw you in so that you have to investigate to find things, but go with what works for you.

You will know whether you have the flow of magic right or not and if you don't, keep tweaking until you do.

A garden altar

Having an outdoor altar is a lovely idea and gives you a magical focal point in the garden. You can use it to leave offerings for the Fae or to deity but also as a focal point to sit outside and meditate in front of. It can be as simple as a flat stone or piece of wood or something grander involving wood, stones, shells and even mirrors and statues. Make sure whatever you place on the altar with the intent of leaving it out is biodegradable and won't harm wildlife if they decide to take a nibble (or your pets). I like to leave natural spells on my garden altar whilst the magic works.

Be creative and use what you have, a few bricks laid together or some old floor tiles would work really well. If you are feeling creative, you could make a mosaic platform using broken tiles or crockery. If you are short of space a shelf on the garden or house wall would also work.

What you put on it is up to you, as always be guided by your intuition. Representations of your gods, the elements and animal spirit guides perhaps?

I found a round paving slab cheaply in a garden centre last year, it has the compass points set into it and it works perfectly as a garden altar.

Spells that work with the elements of nature can be left on the garden altar. Leaves with wishes written on can be left out for the sun to dry. Write spells in chalk on slate or stones and leave them out for the rain to wash them. Paper petitions can be set out to be worked on by the weather too. Draw symbols and sigils in the soil. And of course spells can be buried in your garden as well.

Statues and plaques add another dimension to the garden. I also have a couple of big mirrors against the wall which reflect back images of the plants, but also make the garden look bigger.

You will often find green men (and green lady) plaques in garden centres. We even found a stone wizard statue recently, Steve (the wizard) now presides over one of the flower beds. Wind chimes are a beautiful addition to gardens and can even be hung on balconies and in windows. The sound they make ranges from light tinkly noises from the small metal ones to a deep hollow sound from the bamboo type.

Strings of beads and coloured glass can be hung from branches to create interest and reflections. Solar fairy lights are an excellent electricity/battery free option and can be strung across balconies or in the branches of trees and bushes.

Hex signs

American folk magic has hex signs but they aren't bad or evil, they are a form of protection, good luck and prosperity. They are often geometric in shape and usually very pretty, a lot of them bear a resemblance to mandalas. They are hung outside or just inside the home to bring peace, love and prosperity to the home and to keep out bad luck.

Some symbols used in hex signs and their meanings

Tulip – faith, hope and charity,
Five-point star – protection, good luck,
Triple five-point star – luck, love and happiness,
Rosette – good health and protection from disease,
Oak leaves – strength in mind, body and character,
Hearts – love,
Six-point star – protection referred to in German as hexefus which translated means 'witch's foot'.

Colours are important too – pretty much the same correspondences as we use in colour magic.

Funnily enough some of the old hex signs were used to ward against Witches …

You could paint a hex sign on your garden wall or on a paving slab. Work the design into a mosaic or paint one on a plate to hang on the wall of your house or garden fence. It could even become the focal point of your garden design.

Harvesting

With a veritable smorgasbord of magical ingredients on your doorstep, please remember to ask permission before taking anything from the plants.

If I cut a rose to put on my altar I ask the rose plant first and tell it what the flower will be used for.

If I have harvested lots of herbs I talk to the plant as I cut and then thank it afterwards.

If you are trimming branches or cutting back plants, make sure you know what you are doing. There are really useful sources on the net with advice or check the local library. You can damage or kill plants by pruning incorrectly.

If you have the space it pays to have a water butt, even a small one. We have a bucket under the downspout of our conservatory as we don't have room for a full-size water butt. Rain water is so much better for the plants than tap water. Even though we drink the tap water!

Having water in the garden is a bonus not only for the birds and wildlife. Even if it is just a small pond, the wildlife will arrive all by itself as if by magic.

If you really don't have room for a pond, a bird bath can provide the element of water. You can also get very small bird baths that hang from a tree branch.

Insects can be encouraged into your garden too, not the aphid type because they are pesky 'lil beggars. But bees and hover flies will come for the flowers and can be encouraged to stay by building bug hotels. Just a little space in a corner can be filled with small pieces of wood and twigs to provide hidey holes.

I am often asked what my core choice of herbs would be in the garden. I grow thyme, bay, rosemary, sage, hyssop, lavender, borage, marjoram, chives, mint and lemon balm. I use these a lot in my cooking but also for magical workings. My next go-to magical ingredients are rose petals and poppy heads, not herbs but equally edible and also mainstays in my magical workings.

Your magical store cupboard

I have included lots of correspondence lists within this book (and in various others of mine) and the internet is full of them. Ultimately the Kitchen Witch will use whatever they have to hand.

Use what is in season.

Use what you have in your cupboards.

Use what you have in your own garden.

Use what you find in your local hedgerows.

Create your own correspondences for the herbs and plants you grow yourself.

Pick a leaf or a flower and hold it, connect with the energy it provides and see what it can offer you. Make a note of any words, sentences, feelings or images you receive.

Next time you want to work some magic, go into your garden or your cupboard with the intent in mind. Ask what plant, herb or spice you need and see which one catches your eye.

Make it personal, what works for someone else may not work for you, and vice versa. Trust your intuition and get to know your own plants.

Garden journal

I openly admit I am hopeless at keeping a journal. I buy lots of very pretty notebooks with the good intention of keeping a journal but end up using them for jotting down notes, lists, ideas, recipes and ultimately as I am doing right now – writing books and blog posts in them. I handwrite my books and then type them up ... yes, I know it is labour intensive, but it is just how I roll.

However, we do have a journal for our garden. Actually, it is a spreadsheet on the computer but with the same principal. We record each plant we buy and when we plant it, we also make a note of when it needs pruning or cutting back and the best way and time to propagate it. That way we can keep a record of how old the plants are, what care they need and we know each month which jobs need to be done.

Doctrine of signatures

The widespread belief beginning in the Middle Ages (I don't remember the exact date, even I am not that old) was that natural plants and flowers resembled the part of the body that they could cure or heal (although the idea was probably around a long while before then). The claim was that whatever ceity/ divine being created the plant made the flower, leaf or seed look like the body part that the illness or disease was found in and that it could be used to cure the ailment.

The pretty eyebright plant is a good example, the flower looks like a blue eye, so the plant was used to treat ailments of the eye. Bloodroot has a red extract, so it was used to fix blood problems whereas common purslane stalks looked like worms so were used to treat worms in humans.

This idea became known as the 'doctrine of signatures'. Jakob Boehme published his book on the subject in 1621 titled *Signature of all things* and the botanist William Cole was believed to have said:

> Though Sin and Satan have plunged mankinde into an Ocean of Infirmities, yet the Mercy of God, which is over all his workes, maketh Grasse to grow upon the Mountaines and Herbes for the use of men, and hath not only stamped upon them a distinct forme but also hath given them particular Signatures whereby a man may read the use of them.

Please note: Although some of these plants are often used in herbal medicines (and they will work) it can be a very dangerous occupation to guess purely based on the shape of the plant. Always consult a qualified herbalist before ingesting any herbal remedies. However, I do think this idea can work very well when using magical herbs and plants. Your intent can be carried within the plant by association of the shape or colour.

Gratitude

When we work spells, I think there has to be a thank you involved. If the magic works and the gods have granted our request I do believe it is only polite to say thanks. Working, tending and looking after your garden is an excellent way to do that. You are giving your time, effort and energy to look after nature whether that is the plants, the soil, the insects or birds and animals in your garden.

If your garden is giving you beautiful plants, flowers and trees and providing you with magical, medicinal and culinary ingredients it is only fair that you give something back.

You could perform regular gratitude rituals or make offerings at your garden altar. But think along practical lines as well. Feed and nourish the soil regularly with liquid feed or mulches and compost. Add crystals and other natural offerings of thanks. Sow seeds to replace plants you have harvested.

Recycle and use whatever you take from your garden especially if you have a glut of produce or seedlings. Share them with your friends and neighbours. And don't forget to say thank you to the plant and the earth when you harvest anything.

Devas, dryads, plant and tree spirits

All plants have spirits, and to connect with the magical property of each plant it is my suggestion that you talk to the spirit within it, make a connection. This is easily done, if you don't mind the neighbours thinking you are slightly mad.

Every single plant, tree, herb and flower will have its own very individual and unique energy. That energy can be used for magical or medicinal purposes. But you can also connect with the plant spirit and use its energies for healing, knowledge or seeking answers to questions. Even if you just want to ask why the plant is poorly, not growing well or whether it has enough water.

If you want to find out what magical property a particular herb or plant you have in front of you has, there is a very simple way … ask it! Calm and centre yourself, have the plant or herb in front of you and slowly bring your hands up and towards the plant, as you do so ask (out loud or in your mind) if you can connect with the plant's energy (its aura if you like). As your hands get closer to the plant you should start to fill a resistance coming from the 'bubble' that is the plant's energy field. As you connect with this energy ask what magical properties it holds, hopefully your intuition will answer you.

You can connect with plant spirit guides in various ways. Dreams and meditations are the easiest way to meet your plant ally. Before you go to sleep put out the intent that you would like to meet a plant spirit guide, in particular YOUR plant spirit guide. You will often find that in your dream you will see a plant, tree or flower or you might smell the scent of an herb or even just hear the name of a plant mentioned in your dream. This will often be backed up by seeing the same plant the following day whilst out and about or on the television or in a book.

If you prefer to meditate, set out the intent that you want

to meet your plant spirit guide before you make yourself comfortable, close your eyes and focus on your breathing, then see where your mind takes you and what landscape it leads you to.

The word 'deva' may have originated in Persia and migrated to Greece and then onto the rest of Europe. The word 'deva' is Sanskrit and means 'shining one', this may refer to the aura that is said to shine around the plant that is being worked with. A deva is a plant guardian, but it also has other tasks such as healing plants, helping them grow and protecting and nurturing a whole area of plant life - basically they are nature's architects.

Anyone who works with the animism belief (as I do) will discover tree spirits. Animism is 'the attribution of a living soul to plants, inanimate objects, and natural phenomena'. The word animism is derived from the Latin word 'anima' which means 'breath' or 'soul'. It is the belief that a soul or spirit exists in every object whether it is an animal, plant or rock.

The belief that spirits (or ghosts as they were sometimes believed to be) lived in trees goes back a long way, the Old Testament has references to sacred groves.

Celts, Romans and Egyptians, amongst other cultures all believed in tree spirits. In fact, in India the banyan tree is especially sacred, and shrines are built under the trees to honour the spirit that dwells within.

If you look up the dictionary definition of the word 'dryad' it says: 'in folklore and Greek mythology – a nymph inhabiting a tree or wood', which is just about spot on. Each tree will have its own inner spirit as all plants do, but tree spirits are specifically named dryads.

Greek mythology tells us of dryads, hamadryades and oreads – female nature spirits that dwell within trees, woodlands, groves and forests with a particular fondness for oak trees. All the texts and images from mythology seem to depict dryads as female.

A hamadryade is born with the tree and bound to it for the entire life span of the tree, when the tree dies so does the hamadryade.

Dryads can be found within their own tree or very close by, as they never venture far from it. They are incredibly shy and if startled will quickly disappear into the tree.

In Celtic mythology you will find the same spirits but with different names such as tree nymphs, sidhe draoi or faerie druids. The world of Fairy is vast and there are many, many different types of Fae associated with trees and woodlands.

Mythology and folklore has an enormous number of stories and details for dryads and tree spirits, if you are interested it is a fascinating subject to do some research on.

Design a structure

I like to start with the larger items and work downwards.

Trees provide structure and height and if you go for fruit or nut trees you get the added bonus of an edible harvest. They also provide roosting and nesting places for birds. Perhaps an obvious thing to say but trees grow, some of them to great heights. Choose a tree that is suitable for the size of your garden. You can get a lot of trees now that are grafted onto dwarf root stock (not elemental dwarves obviously because that would make them extremely grumpy ...). These provide the small garden with access to fruit trees and even something like a small willow. Trust me, I speak from experience – you don't want to be chopping down a tree that has grown too large and digging out the roots because it is not only a lot of hard work but also heartbreaking.

Next come the shrubs and again some of these grow quite large so choose carefully. Birds also like to nest in shrubs. A lot of shrub varieties also provide the bonus of being evergreen and/or providing year-round interest in the form of leaves, flowers and berries (also food for the birds).

Perennials are those plants that come back each year and can often be divided in the spring or autumn to provide extra plants. Although a lot of these do die right back over winter they are (hopefully) reborn again each spring.

Annuals only last the summer and are often used for bedding and hanging baskets. They are easily grown from seed and you can usually collect seed for the following year once they have finished flowering. Hybrids may not come true from seed, although you will get flowers they may not be the exact colour, but that's all part of the adventure!

For the most part herbs tend to be perennial but it will depend on the area/zone you live in. A lot of herbs hail from the Mediterranean and require warmer temperatures and they usually like very well-drained soil.

If you are lucky Mother Nature will also come into play with some plants by self-seeding, whether carried on the wind or dropped by birds. I have borage, poppies, foxgloves and love-in-a-mist that appear all over the garden in random places. I have a holly tree that grew from a seed that arrived in the form of a bird poop. He had obviously not long snacked on a belly full of holly berries!

I wholeheartedly encourage you to experiment with your garden; you don't know how well something will grow until you try it, although doing your research first will help hugely. You will have some astounding successes but also a few spectacular failures. But unless you try you won't know.

What you grow will obviously depend a great deal on your soil type, area and aspect but consider these groups:

Aesthetic: Plants you actually love the look of whether it is the flower or leaf colour and shape or the structure of the whole plant.

Aromatic: There are so many amazing scented plants, not only herbs but flowers. This may be because you love the smell but can also be grown for aromatherapy purposes.

Culinary: Edibles for putting in the pot – casserole or teapot.

Lotions and potions: Grown for you to create lotions and body treatments such as herbal shampoo, soap and body scrubs.

Magical: Grown specifically for their magical properties and to use in your crafting and spell work.

Medicinal: Grow these to use in tinctures, balms, salves and herbal medicines. Note: Please make sure you identify correctly any plant that you intend to ingest. If using medically please consult a qualified professional first. Herbal medicines can be incredibly powerful and can clash badly with over-the-counter medicines.

Pick a theme, any theme

Themed gardens can be fun to design. Obviously if you have a large plot you could put several different themed areas in (I can but dream ...). Even if your garden is small you can always dedicate one corner to a theme. There are plenty of ideas to choose from but here are some suggestions to get you started.

A dark and deadly place

Let's start with a wicked witch's garden and by wicked, I mean just a witch, coz we are nice people really. There are plenty of baneful plants to work with. Please be careful when dealing with these plants, some are highly toxic to humans and pets. Even if you don't ingest them some can be skin irritants. If you or anyone accidentally eats any part of the plant, seek medical attention immediately.

There are some beautiful plants included here and it would make a fascinating display.

I think we need to look at the word baneful, the dictionary lists it as: *'destructive; pernicious; exceedingly harmful; deadly; poisonous; causing harm, death or ruin'*.

It seems this cheerful term first came into use during the 1500s and it appears on quite a few of our herbs and plants; dogbane, fleabane, henbane, witchbane and wolfsbane, for example.

At one point in history these herbs were used to inflict pain or even death on others alongside creating potions to induce visions, to force the will of another or altered states of mind (sometimes permanently altered). The chemical makeup of these plants can produce hallucinations or death, please be extremely careful.

Flying ointment

One of the most well-known uses for baneful plants was for flying ointments. A salve that was made by adding plant matter to fat which was then rubbed on the body to induce an hallucination that allowed the person to believe they were flying. This is not a recommended course of action, really it isn't – slathering your skin with poisonous ingredients is not wise. If you want an out of body experience then please do try the method of astral projection, it is so much safer and doesn't involve covering yourself in deadly animal fat.

Many stories are told of witches creating magic potions that would allow them to fly and the ingredients were said to be mixed with the fat from plump human babies ... Do remember that our ancestors were wary of anyone that appeared to be different or have magical abilities – and that included the herbalists who could cure illness and disease. They also liked to sit and gossip, in fact a lot of people still do.

Historians have found details on flying ointments that included herbs from the nightshade family such as belladonna, datura, mandrake and henbane with the addition of less poisonous, but still dangerous plants like mugwort and poppies.

The practice of using hallucinogenic plants isn't restricted to witches. The history of their use goes back thousands of years and includes Shamanic and Native American tribes whose rituals included experiencing trance journeys.

I believe that if you study hard and work at your Craft then you can reach a trance state for journeying without the need to endanger your health or your life messing about with poisons, but that is purely my own point of view.

You can, however, create a salve or an incense to help create a good atmosphere for astral travel or Otherworld journeys without the use of poisonous or hallucinogenic plants. Play around with some of your favourite herbs and spices or use those that are particularly associated with astral travel, psychic abilities, meditation or the Otherworld such as:

Bay, beech, benzoin, black pepper, blackthorn, borage, cat nip, chamomile, cinnamon, dandelion, eucalyptus, fennel, fenugreek, frankincense, jasmine, juniper, marigold, myrrh, mugwort, parsley, pine, rose, white and red sandalwood, star anise, thyme and yarrow.

Or you could create a medicine pouch which includes baneful plants, that way you benefit from their spirit rather than choking on fumes from burning them.

Flying ointment salve (a safe one)

2 cups of oil such as olive, almond or coconut
¼ cup beeswax chips
4-6 teaspoons of your chosen dried herbs (I like a mixture of
    red sandalwood, bay and mugwort)

Heat the oil in a pan with the herbs over a low heat, preferably in a double boiler for two to three hours until the oil takes on a green colour. Or you can pop the herbs into the oil in a jar with a lid and leave for three to four weeks, shaking daily. You will need to do one of these methods to infuse the herbs into the oil.

Strain the herbs from the oil. Add the oil to a double boiler with the beeswax chips until they have melted. Pour into small pots or jars and pop on the lids.

If you prefer not to use beeswax then candelilla wax can be substituted but you may need to adjust the quantity and use slightly less candelilla wax than you would beeswax.

If you want to create your salve with soy wax, use these quantities plus your chosen herbs.

1 cup soy wax
1½ cups oil

You may also need to add a tablespoon or two of water to create the right consistency.

Flying incense blend

Equal quantities of each:

Benzoin

Cinnamon

Sandalwood

Pine

Astral travel tea herbs

You could use just one of the following or a blend, but they may all assist in astral travel:

Cinnamon, chamomile, echinacea, eucalyptus, ginger, ginseng, mint, lavender, mugwort, primrose, valerian and willow.

Baneful plant suggestions

Aconite – Always wear gloves when handling this plant, the poison can be absorbed through the skin; one of the original flying ointment ingredients.

Angel's trumpet – don't be fooled by the name ... the whole plant is poisonous.

Belladonna – also known as nightshade or deadly nightshade. It is highly toxic; one of the original ingredients in flying ointment.

Bloodroot (tetterwort) – this plant is not edible, it contains toxic alkaloids which if ingested can cause severe irritation or in a large enough dose, fatality. It is used in some herbal remedies, but I advise only doing so if you are a qualified herbalist.

Caster bean – said to be one of the most poisonous plants in the world, all parts of the plant are toxic especially the seeds.

Datura – all the plants in this species are poisonous with

the seeds and flowers being the most toxic parts; another original ingredient from flying ointment.

Delphinium – the poison in delphinium is most toxic when the plant is young, they can also irritate the skin.

Dogsbane – it has toxic side effects, do not ingest.

Elder – this one may come as a surprise as we collect the flowers and berries from the elder for culinary use. However, the unripe berries are toxic, cooking them makes them edible. The leaves, seeds and wood are all toxic.

Fleabane – as the name suggests, it is an insect repellent plant, however, it can be poisonous to some animals such as cattle.

Foxglove – a seemingly harmless plant grown in many gardens (mine included). It is used in heart medicine but is very toxic.

Gloriosa – also called flame lily. The whole plant is poisonous.

Hellebore – this beautiful plant has an eerie feel to it, a spring flower that loves to sit in the shade. Once used to cure insanity (apparently), I suspect that rather than the cure it was the cause, as this plant is very toxic.

Hemlock – a common name for a group of plants (poison hemlock, water hemlock and water dropworts to name a few). This plant is definitely poisonous, as Socrates can confirm ...

Henbane – Every single part of this plant is toxic. Use in magical workings for binding, spirit work and Otherworld connections.

Jessamine – also called woodbine. All parts of jessamine are toxic.

Larkspur – parts of this plant are highly toxic.

Lily of the valley – don't be fooled by the small delicate appearance of this plant as it is toxic, and those toxins can be absorbed through the skin.

Mandrake – quite a toxic plant it has long been used in magic particularly for love spells.

May apple – also called American mandrake. The whole plant is toxic including the sap, so don't get it on your skin.

Mistletoe – mistletoe seems to choose where it wants to live whether you like it or not. There are an enormous number of species in the mistletoe family but only a few of them are toxic and you do have to eat quite a lot of it to become ill but better not to chance it!

Nicotiana – Obviously this plant contains nicotine which we know is not good for our bodies but eating it rather than smoking it can be highly toxic even fatal.

Oleander – the sap is incredibly irritating to the skin and all parts of the plant are highly toxic even after drying.

Pokeweed – a plant generally found in the USA, the whole plant is toxic.

Yew – the Yew tree is one of death and rebirth and a wonderful tree to have in your garden, but they are highly toxic.

Witchbane – can be a strong irritant to the skin.

Wolfsbane (also known as monkshood) – wear gloves when handling as the plant contains a poisonous alkaloid.

Wormwood – even the name sounds baneful. This was one of the ingredients in the extremely powerful alcoholic drink absinthe, but large quantities can be extremely toxic (the absinthe and wormwood). Drinking absinthe is like swallowing paint stripper, trust me.

For magical uses these plants could be included:

To send negative intent and energy back to its source...
Agrimony, ginger, mullein, nettle, rue, thistle.

Deflection against ill intent...
Blackthorn, elder, ginger, mullein, nettle, pennyroyal, pepper, rue, willow, star anise.

Return negative intent and energy back to the sender and keep it there...
Blackthorn, elder, rue, willow.

Cursing, I don't mean rude words (although you might like to add them), I mean sending curses and hexes...
Cypress, dragon's blood, rowan, wormwood, yarrow.

Seasonal garden

Generally, people seem to design gardens to have year-round interest and that totally makes sense, but it can also be an interesting project to have a seasonal garden. One designed to shine in spring, autumn or even winter. Or you could divide your garden into four and have different sections for each season. If you prefer year-round colour, then maybe divide the garden into four and have each section a distinct colour to represent each season? Yellow for spring, red for summer, orange for autumn and white for winter perhaps? There are also plants that give continuous year-round colour.

Obviously, it will depend on your climate and the weather in your area as to what flowers when, and I am positive that Mother Nature is menopausal now as the seasons seem to be all over the place.

Spring plants

Spring is a time for the flowering bulbs to shine but remember they take a bit of thinking ahead as most of them must be planted the autumn before. Suggested bulbs and spring flowering plants:

Crocus, daffodil, tulip, fritillary, lily of the valley, hyacinth, winter aconite, bluebells, puschkinia, pleione, lungwort (pulmonaria), bishop's hat (epimedium), wallflower (erysimum), alpine wood fern, Siberian squill, cyclamen, clematis (look for the spring flowering varieties, arrowwood (viburnum), winter daphne, Siberian bugloss, violets, winter pansies, wood anemone, bleeding heart, spurge, magnolia, polystichums, euphorbia, periwinkle, primula, allium, hellebore, aubretia, aquilegia (columbine), forsythia, bloodroot and wisteria.

Summer plants

You are spoilt for choice during the summer with all the annuals and bedding plants, visit your local plant nursery to see what is best but here are some suggestions:

Delphinium, Foxglove, Lilies, Crocosmia, Sedum, Hosta, Monarda, Aagapanthus, geranium, pelargonium, lavender, dahlia, hydrangea, achillea, peony, roses, clematis, phlox, daisy, salvia, coreopsis, buddleia, marigolds, penstemon, zinnia, bougainvillea, hibiscus and gaillardia.

Autumn plants

With the right conditions a lot of the summer flowering plants will continue their show throughout the autumn as well. I have even had pelargoniums and roses flowering through until December! Some of my recommendations are late summer flowers that continue into autumn. Some suggestions:

Chrysanthemum, cyclamen, anemone, dahlia, knautia, eryngium, nerine, exochorda, rudbeckia, aster, ribes, salvia, penstemon, hollyhock, geum, berberis, cosmos, maura, cotoneaster, Michaelmas daisy, sunflower, coneflower, plumbago, kniphofia, salvia, vervain, bergamot, phlox, monkshood and smoke tree.

Winter plants

There are some beautiful plants that flower or bring colour to a winter garden, here are some suggestions:

Heather, Japanese quince, winter aconites, cyclamen, viburnum, hellebore, winter pansy, winter flowering cherry, mahonia, dogwood, snowdrops, witch hazel, winter jasmine, crocus, chionodoxa, daphne, clematis cirrhosa, iris, skimmia japonica, sarcococca, hyacinth and bergenia.

All-year colour plants

Some plants are evergreen providing year-round colour and others provide beautiful coloured bark or stems. There are some lovely shrubs where the flowers are followed by berries that bring extra colour too. Others will have flowers in the summer followed by fantastic seed heads that stay in shape right throughout the winter. Some suggestions:

Trachelospermum jasminoides, Amelanchier lamarckii, acer, birch, echinacea, heuchera, sedum, lots of the ornamental grasses, dogwood, bergenia, camellia, box, geranium, photinia, choisya, nandina, pittosporum, sempervivium, cordyline, pieris, juniper and bay.

Sabbat garden

Divide your garden or plot into eight and put plants, ornaments and decorations in each section to represent the sabbats. You could work this so the plants flower in each season, but it will mean parts of the garden will look fairly empty at certain times of the year, which if you are Okay with then no problem. You could help by having a main structure throughout it all using evergreen shrubs and plants then weaving seasonal plants through each section. Alternatively, you could make each section a different colour to represent each sabbat:

Green and reds for the winter solstice (Yule),
Whites and pale yellows for Imbolc,
Blues and pinks for the spring equinox (Ostara),

Oranges and reds for Beltane,
Explosion of colours for the summer solstice (Litha),
Yellows for Lughnasadh,
Oranges for the autumn equinox (Mabon),
Blacks and orange for Samhain.

Samhain

Bay, broom, catnip, garlic, heather, mandrake, mugwort, mullein, nettle, oak, passion flower, pine, rosemary, rue, sage, sunflower, wormwood.

Yule/Winter Solstice

Birch, cedar, elder, hazel, holly, ivy, mistletoe, oak, pine, rose, sandalwood.

Imbolc

Ash, basil, celandine, chamomile, coriander, garlic, heather, rosemary, sage, witch hazel, vervain, violet.

Ostara/Spring Equinox

Broom, celandine, cinquefoil, crocus, daffodil, dogwood, elder, honeysuckle, jasmine, lavender, lemon balm, lily of the valley, lilac, lovage, marjoram, meadowsweet, oak, rose, tansy, thyme, tulip, violet, vervain, willow.

Beltane

Ash, broom, cinquefoil, coriander, daffodil, dogwood, elder, fern, flax, hawthorn, marigold, marjoram, meadowsweet, nettle, self-heal, rose, rue, snapdragon, thistle, woodruff.

Litha/Summer Solstice

Basil, chamomile, cinquefoil, elder, fennel, fern, feverfew, hazel, heather, honeysuckle, hyssop, iris, lavender, meadowsweet, mistletoe, mugwort, oak, pansy, parsley, pine, rosemary, rowan, rue, sage, Saint John's wort, sunflower, thyme, vervain.

Lughnasadh/Lammas

Aloe, basil, blackthorn, clover, comfrey, elder, garlic, goldenrod, heather, heliotrope, ivy, marigold, meadowsweet, mint, mugwort, myrtle, peony, poppy, rose, sunflower, vervain, yarrow.

Mabon/Autumn Equinox

Chamomile, fern, marigold, mistletoe, oak, passionflower, rosemary, rue, sage, sunflower, thistle, walnut, yarrow.

Container garden

There are some plants that I always grow in pots such as lemon balm and mint, particularly because if let loose in the garden they are total thugs and completely take over. I also have lots of pots for annuals in the summer. But if you have a small courtyard garden or an area that is solid concrete or a patio, you can work solely with containers, from small pots to large built raised beds. It also means you can re-arrange the display easily and rotate plants in season. You can also move them out of the way once they are past their best. Even vegetables can be grown in containers.

The key factor is proper drainage and you will have to feed and water them regularly during the summer months. Raising containers up on small bricks or pebbles can also help with the drainage.

Tight on space garden

City witches may be limited on space and those living in apartments may only have a balcony or window sill. Never fear! You can still work garden magic. Lots of plants and herbs do really well in pots on a window sill and balconies can be filled with containers and window boxes (please check the structural strength first). If you have steps up to your apartment you can even stand pots on either side of the steps.

You will have to be creative and experiment. Light levels and shade will affect what you can grow, and everything will need to be watered and fed regularly.

Vertical gardens work very well if you are limited for space. These utilise walls. Fix boxes, troughs and brackets to put pots on and hang baskets from. Create wall 'shelves' by fixing old wooden pallets to walls or literally fix shelves so that you can have lots of levels of plants without the need for floor space.

Tuck succulents and herbs into the slats of old wooden shutters fixed to a wall or fence.

Make canvas/sacking pockets and fill with soil to hang from walls or fences.

With window boxes you can grow lots of different plants, event vegetables with a bit of effort. Be careful and make sure they are fixed properly and watch out when watering. No one wants a box falling on their head or a shower from a watering can.

Stepladders make creative 'stepped' (pun intended) plant stands for small spaces and can be painted to brighten up dark corners.

In fact, old furniture makes very good plant holders. I have seen dressers and cabinets in gardens with drawers full of plants and herbs. We have an old wrought iron bed head in our garden for a climber to ramble through.

Large pots with tall plants can be used to divide sections of the garden, create a 'wall' or hide things such as dustbins.

Use any containers you have, just drill a couple of holes in the bottom if they don't have drainage. Old pots and pans, buckets, boots, wooden crates, baskets, casserole dishes, tin cans, reusable shopping bags, dustbin/trash cans, colanders, watering cans and even old wheelbarrows can be utilised.

Suggested container plants

Patio roses are designed to live in pots and some of the shrub varieties are good too.

Violas/pansies provide seasonal colour.

Heucheras provide beautiful coloured foliage for containers.

Begonias provide good foliage and flower colour during the summer.

Coleus has amazing coloured foliage in the summer (pollinators also love the tiny flowers).

Nemesia has tons of flowers throughout the summer, treated usually as an annual.

Hydrangea is one of the few shrubs that is happy in a pot, particularly the dwarf varieties and you can control the specific soil it likes too. The flowers also dry well.

Petunias throw a big splash of colour in upright and trailing varieties.

Hibiscus in its tree form looks glorious in a container and it can be underplanted with annuals.

Most herbs are happy in a pot; in fact some are better in pots such as mint or lemon balm so that they don't take over the garden. I have two bay trees in pots that are growing away quite happily.

Canna lilies look stunning in a pot and can be taken indoors easily to overwinter.

Ornamental grasses give height and most live well in a container. We have three 'fairy tale' grasses in pots that are extremely happy.

Phormiums come in beautiful shades of foliage; we have a deep burgundy leaf phormium in a contrasting yellow sandstone pot that looks wonderful.

Ferns can be put in pots to fill up shady corners of the garden.

Lavender grows well in pots; in fact I have to grow mine in a pot because it doesn't like our heavy clay soil.

Yuccas make striking plants for pots and can be underplanted with seasonal annuals.

Boxwood is a lovely evergreen for containers.

Pieris has beautiful foliage and flowers in the spring.

Bergenia has excellent foliage and pink blossoms.

Dogwood brings out stunning coloured stems in the winter.

Hostas work well in containers and help to deter the slugs unless they are mountaineering experts (I have had some of those in our garden).

Some of the hebes grow happily in containers.

Some of the smaller Japanese maples (Acers) lend themselves well to containers.

Also, dahlias, pelargoniums, fuchsia, bulbs such as daffodil, tulip and crocus, abutilon, aster, azalea, camellia, cistus, cotoneaster, daphne, escallonia, forsythia, wintergreen, gardenia, gaura, dwarf holly, dwarf lilac, dwarf magnolia, peony, potentilla, dwarf spirea, astilbe, bleeding hearts, chrysanthemum, coreopsis, sedum, verbena and yarrow.

Annuals – there are a wide variety of annuals, bedding and trailing plants that can be used during the summer for pots, baskets and boxes. Check out your local plant nursery to see what is on offer.

Fruit – lots of fruit can be grown in containers just make sure you have enough plants to pollinate each other and that they are compatible, if they aren't self-pollinators. Most plant nurseries now supply fruit trees on dwarf root stock so that they don't grow too big; these are perfect for growing in pots. Apples, apricots, blueberries, cherries, figs, grapes, nectarines, lemons, olives, peaches, pears and plums all do well in containers. They will need plenty of water during the summer months.

Vegetables – a lot can be grown easily in pots, baskets or sacks. Strawberries, cherry tomatoes and herbs can all be grown successfully in hanging baskets. Lettuce, cabbage, squash, potatoes, beans, peas, cucumbers, radish, broccoli, beets, onions, carrots, aubergine/eggplant and peppers all grow happily in containers. The beans and peas will need supports to grow up obviously.

I think the only real way to know if a plant works in a container is to try it!

Intent garden

You could create areas in your garden that are organised by intent. A protection area, a love nest, healing or prosperity section maybe. As each plant has one or more magical properties (usually several) you can grow plants as individual spells or create an entire bed with a specific intent.

Seeds also work well as growing spells. Plant the seed with your intent and then add your energy to it each day to keep the spell going.

Prosperity garden

This might include lots of green foliage, green being a colour of money. Add in orange flowers for success and maybe plants that have lots of seeds such as fennel, seeds being good for prosperity. Grow plants that are associated with the magical correspondences of money and prosperity such as:

Ash, basil, bergamot (orange), calamus, camellia, cedar, chamomile, clover, comfrey, dill, dock, fenugreek, ginger, goldenrod, gorse, hazel, honeysuckle, honesty, jasmine, mandrake, mint, myrtle, nettle, oak, patchouli, periwinkle, poppy, skullcap, tulip, vervain and woodruff.

It's a love thang garden

This is a wonderful theme to work with; not only could you include plants that correspond with love (see suggestions below) but you could work with a pink and red colour theme or even just one plant such as the rose but in all different colours.

Agrimony, ash, aster, basil, betony, birch, bleeding heart, catnip, chamomile, chestnut, chickweed, cinquefoil, cleavers, clover, coltsfoot, columbine (aquilegia), coriander, cornflower, crocus, cyclamen, daffodil, daisy, dandelion, dill, dittany of Crete, dock, elm, fern, geranium, ginger, hawthorn, hazel, heather, horehound, hyacinth, iris, ivy, jasmine, juniper, lady's mantle, lavender, lemon balm, lilac, lobelia, lovage, mallow, mandrake, marjoram, meadowsweet, mistletoe, myrtle, orchid, pansy, passion flower, periwinkle, poppy, primrose, rose, rosemary, rowan, Saint John's wort, sea holly, sorrel, thyme, tulip, valerian, vervain, violet, willow, yarrow.

Healing garden

This idea can be a combination of medicinal plants that can be turned into medicines but also created for a healing atmosphere to sit and be calming and soothing.

Anemone, angelica, ash, bay, blackthorn, bluebell, bracken, burdock, calamus, carnation, coltsfoot, comfrey, coriander, cowslip, cramp bark, dock, echinacea, elder, eucalyptus, fennel, feverfew, garlic, hazel, horehound, hyssop, ivy, juniper, knotweed, lemon balm, lungwort, marjoram, mint, mistletoe, mugwort, nettle, oak, pine, plantain, rose, rosemary, rowan, rue, Saint John's wort, sorrel, tansy, thistle, thyme, vervain, violet, willow.

Protection garden

Gardens at the front of the house are ideal for protection themes. Either design a whole garden with protection in mind or just add protection plants by your doorway, pathways and gates.

African violet, agrimony, aloe, alyssum, anemone, angelica, ash, aster, basil, bay, benzoin, betony, birch, blackthorn, bluebell, borage, bracken, broom, burdock, buttercup, calamus, carnation, cedar, celandine, chickweed, chrysanthemum, cinquefoil, clover, comfrey, coriander, cornflower, cramp bark, cyclamen, cypress, daffodil, daisy, datura, delphinium, dill, dittany of Crete, dogwood, elder, fennel, fern, feverfew, foxglove, garlic, geranium, gorse, gourd, grass, hawthorn, hazel, heather, heliotrope, holly, honeysuckle, horehound, hyssop, ivy, juniper, lavender, lilac, lily, lobelia, lovage, mallow, mandrake, marigold, marjoram, mint, mistletoe, mugwort, mustard, myrtle, nettle, oak, parsley, pennyroyal, peony, periwinkle, pine, plantain, primrose, rose, rosemary, rowan, rue, sage, Saint John's wort, self-heal, snapdragon, Solomon's seal, sunflower, sweet pea, tansy, thistle, tulip, valerian, vervain, violet, willow, witch hazel, woodruff, wormwood, yarrow.

Sun garden

This idea lends itself to sunflowers as the centre and they come in all shapes and sizes, but any bright yellow and orange flowers would work well. Particularly suited are those flowers that open in the sun or follow the sun as it traverses across the sky. You could also include 'desert' type plants with shingle, stones and succulents (bear in mind that a lot of succulents are not frost hardy).

The flowers that open in the sun and close at night tend to do so as a survival instinct to protect them from nocturnal insects. It helps retain moisture within the plant along with protecting them against the drop in temperature during the night. Suggested 'sun opening' plants:

Moring glory, gazania, California poppy, chickweed, rose of Sharon, magnolia (grandiflora), mesembryanthemum, purple winecup, bloodroot, sacred lotus and scarlet pimpernel.

Heliotropism is the seasonal motion of flowers or leaves in response to the direction of the sun. Heliotropium translates as 'sunturn'. Renamed phototropism in the late 1800s as it was recognised that the plant responds to light levels rather than specifically following the sun.

Some flowers are perfectly suited to full sun such as:

Adenium, artemisia, Asiatic lily, bearded iris, bottlebrush, calliandra, canna, celosia, coneflowers, coreopsis, cuphea, day lilies, dianthus, delphinium, delosperma, echinacea, gaillardia, hibiscus, ixora, lantana, marigold, nasturtiums, pelargonium, pentas, peony, petunia, plumbago, portulaca, red hot poker, rudbeckia, salvia, sedum, verbena and yarrow.

Or you could include plants that are ruled by the Sun, such as:

Angelica, ash, bay, bergamot, buttercup, calamus, carnation, cedar, celandine, chamomile, chrysanthemum, eucalyptus, hazel, heliotrope, juniper, lovage, marigold, mistletoe, morning glory, oak, peony, rosemary, rowan, rue, St John's wort, sunflower, walnut and witch hazel.

You can often find sun design plaques and hanging ornaments which can be also be added.

Moon garden

Moon gardens can have many facets. Using all white and silver plants works well but also plants that flower or release their scent at night. There are many plants that are also associated with the energy of the moon.

Creating moon-shaped flower beds and using white and grey stones, pebbles, crystals and shingle can also be effective. Reflective surfaces can be included, whether it is mirrors, dark pools of water or white candles. Suggested white or silver plants, these all come in white varieties:

Artemisia, astilbe, acanthus, agapanthus, agave, alstroemeria, anemone, angelica, lilies, heliotrope, petunia, scabiosa, wisteria, dianthus, hibiscus, hydrangea, daffodil, magnolia, jasmine, camellia, datura (moonflower), hyacinth, peony, aquilegia/columbine, lilac, chrysanthemum, hellebore, yarrow, cosmos, begonia, ferns, centaurea, cardoon, sea holly, helichrysum, heuchera, brunnera, lungwort, dusty miller, melianthus, curry plant, sedum, dicentra alba, evening primrose, honeysuckle, hosta, maiden grass, moonflowers, nicotiana, sage, clematis, rhododendron, viburnum, cistus, lunaria annua, convolvulus, roses, primula, foxglove, phlox, dahlia, echinacea, tulips, allium, stachys, lavender, grasses, delphinium and white daisies.

Plants that are ruled by the moon:

Aloe, birch, calamus, camellia, chickweed, dittany, eucalyptus, evening primrose, gourd, honesty, hyssop, iris, ivy, jasmine, juniper, lemon balm, lily, mallow, mugwort, myrtle, poppy, rose, sweet pea, willow and wormwood.

Culinary garden

If you want to grow fruit and vegetables but also want to incorporate pretty flowers you can do both. Cottage gardens traditionally had flowers inter-planted with vegetables. However, you could go the whole hog and use totally edible plants, because some flowers are tasty too.

See the section on edible flowers for ideas.

Meditation garden

Create a whole garden for meditation or just a corner for a meditation spot. A shady place works well and if it can be beside water, even better. I like the sound of wind chimes, so they can be hung in the space to create a simple, pleasant noise. Leave some room to set a candle carefully and maybe even some incense or place scented plants around where you would sit. Think about the colour of any plants placed here and perhaps keep them cool and calm shades. If space allows, then a fire pit or basket would also make a good addition.

If you plan on having a garden altar, then a meditation spot is the perfect place for it.

There are certain plants magically associated with mediation such as:

Bergamot, cramp bark, fenugreek, goldenrod, honeysuckle, horseradish, jasmine, lilac, red sandalwood and wormwood.

These can all be grown for your mediation garden, but I think a meditation garden is more about the atmosphere you create. My suggestion is to use a suitable colour palette; mine would be whites and pastel colours. But also including some lightly scented plants too.

Water is a lovely feature for meditating with. The sound of trickling water can be very soothing, or it can make you want to pee, so you will have to see what works for you!

Having a comfy spot to sit is important. It doesn't have to be a grand summer house or tea house, although if you have the space and the budget they are perfect (in my dream world). A bench, a bottom-height wall or even a small patch of grass you can set a cushion on will work. A winding pathway to your meditation spot not only looks good but can help to enter a meditative state as you walk, counting down as you take each step on the pathway.

Some privacy is useful if you can, even a spot screened by a few tall plants in pots such as bamboo or a moveable screen.

I visited a bar in Spain earlier this year (yes, I did have a very large cocktail) it was outside in a walled garden. Huge bean bags and cushions were scattered around, and armchairs set out. There was even a big double iron-frame bed to sit or lay on. The trees around the edge with branches overhead were strung with pretty fairy lights, candles and lanterns. If you took away the bar serving drinks and the party revellers it would have been the perfect spot for meditating, actually on second thoughts leave the bar ...

Lighting can set the mood effectively. Fairy lights in the garden look lovely as do lanterns. Candles are great but be careful to set them in a spot where they won't get knocked over or set fire to anything.

Fire pits, fire baskets, chimeneas or even a cauldron can be used as a focal point for meditation and to throw herbs or incense blends on to. They can also provide heat if you want to sit outside in the evening or wrapped up on a chilly day.

Put scented plants around your meditation area. Things such as cypress, lavender or jasmine work well.

You must create a garden that is peaceful and restful to YOU. Close your eyes and visualise your ideal mediation garden. Or here's a thought ... meditate on it! Jot down the images and ideas you see, then, work out how you can translate them into reality.

If your garden is near a busy, noisy road or factory you may have to think about how to block out the noise. Although the monotonous drone of traffic can be very meditative. Screens, bushes or trees can help.

Take a look at gardens from around the world for inspiration. Japanese gardens often have a lot of Zen elements. A spot filled with gravel or sand for you to draw symbols or patterns in can be therapeutic. However, if you have cat visitors to your garden you may want to cover up the sand pit when not using it ... just saying ...

Think about textures of where you will sit, stand or touch. You need to be able to relax and be comfortable. Sitting on a cold lumpy brick wall is not going to help you get your 'om' on. Soft grasses of all kinds, bricks covered in moss, smooth pavers or a wooden bench will be more comfy.

Sculptures, statues and ornaments can add to the feel. Go with items that speak to you; angels, fairies, goddesses or animals that bring you a sense of peace.

Set up a mediation altar; use a small plank of wood, a few bricks, or a large flat stone. Room to set a candle and some incense maybe. You could also leave offerings and fresh flowers. Sometimes just leaving empty spaces can work as well.

You don't need fancy meditation stools or yoga mats. I have a piece of fabric I like to use as a 'mediation blanket'. Folded up I can sit on it to make sitting on the floor comfortable. Inside I use it as a blanket if I am lying down to journey/hedge ride. A towel or doormat will serve just as well.

If you have the space, you could add a small labyrinth or spiral walkway.

Meditation plant suggestions:

Aloe, roses, jasmine, chamomile, lavender, maples, fruit trees, ferns, grasses, bamboo, rosemary, sage, honeysuckle, patchouli, rue, witch hazel, woodruff, alyssum, cowslip, lungwort, mint, passion flower, self-heal, pine, daisy, eucalyptus, heather, iris, marigold, yarrow, borage, coriander, hyacinth, meadowsweet, sea holly, thyme, valerian and violets.

Garden for children

Children love to mess about in the dirt. When I was young my dad gave us a small section of his allotment to grow things in. When my own children were little, a big section of our garden was turned over to sand pits and children-sized garden furniture with added room for a paddling pool. The plants definitely took a back seat. Sometimes you have to adapt and move with priorities.

Try planting a growing 'tent' by placing sunflower seeds in a square or circle so they grow up to form a flower wall. Get the children involved in planting seeds and plants. Our youngest chose his own hanging basket this year and decided what plants he wanted to put in it.

Lots of bright colours entice children as do little fun statues hidden in amongst the plants. They also like to be hands-on, so use lots of tactile surfaces and materials. Scented plants are also good and ones that have leaves and petals that are soft or furry.

Children also like plants that they can grow and harvest from, such as fruits like strawberries; also get them involved in growing beans and carrots. It may even encourage them to eat their vegetables if they have grown and picked them. Plant suggestions:

Sunflowers, succulents, snapdragons, nasturtiums, marigolds, zinnias, all herbs, beans, radish, tomato, pumpkins, lamb's ear, grasses, Chinese lantern, money plant, primrose, strawberry, campanula, pansy, crane's bill, sempervivum, lavender, Alchemilla mollis, forget me not, sweet pea, lettuce, cosmos, cornflower, tobacco plant, courgette/zucchini, carrot, potato, beetroot, daisies, milkweed, petunia, elephant's ear, allium, chenille, passionflower, sedum, scadoxus, hyacinth, verbascum.

Herbal tea garden

If you love herbal tea what about creating a plot solely dedicated to herbs and flowers that can be used in tea blends? Oh, if only I could have a cake garden to go with it … Set a chair and table in the garden and you could sit in your tea garden drinking your own homegrown tea blend. Lots of herbs and flowers can be used fresh to make herbal tea but others are better dried first.

As a general guide use two tablespoons finely chopped fresh herbs or one tablespoon finely crumbled dried herbs to one mug of water. Boil the water you need and as soon as it boils pour the water onto your herbals. Steep for five minutes. If you prefer a stronger taste add more herbs rather than steeping for longer. Strain and pour. Some of my favourite plants to grow for tea:

Angelica – use the root to aid with digestion. Magical properties: Protection, healing, exorcism, divination, prosperity, luck, hex breaking, courage.

Basil – use a couple of fresh leaves for a refreshing tea. Magical properties: Wealth, money, prosperity, love, exorcism, protection, happiness, peace.

Bergamot (Monarda) – a strong flavour (part of the mint family) you will only need a few leaves. Magical properties: Abundance, meditation, sleep, dreams, clarity, friendship.

Betony – use the leaves for a fragrant tea. Magical properties: Love, purification, clarity, protection, anti-intoxication, nightmares, anti-depression, memory, stress relief.

Catnip – not just for cats! Use the leaves to help bring calm. Magical properties: Love, fertility, cat magic, dreams, happiness, courage.

Chamomile – use the buds to relax and calm and to help you sleep. Magical properties: Sleep, dreams, love, calm, money, relaxation, purification, balancing.

Coriander – the seeds produce a warm citrusy flavour. Magical properties: Health, healing, peace, love, release, wealth, protection, negativity.

Echinacea – use the buds to boost your immune system. Magical properties: Crone magic, power, healing, abundance.

Fennel – use one teaspoon of crushed seeds or a few leaves. Magical properties: Healing, purification, protection, courage, confidence, fertility, initiation.

Ginger – use the sliced root to make a warming tea. Magical properties: Money, success, power, love, cleansing, protection, consecratation.

Lavender – use the buds to soothe. Magical properties: Happiness, peace, love, protection, sleep, clarity, faeries, strength.

Lemon balm – use the leaves for a calming cuppa. Magical properties: Success, healing, anti-depression, memory, love, anxiety.

Lemon verbena – a zesty tea with all sorts of beneficial properties. Magical properties: Nightmares, purification, exorcism, love.

Mint leaves – spearmint will give a different flavour to common mint but also try some of the flavoured mints such as chocolate mint. It is calming and good for digestion. Magical properties: Money, healing, exorcism, protection, cleansing, calming.

Nettles – use the leaves for a detox. Magical properties: Healing, protection, lust, money, exorcism.

Passionflower – use the leaves to relax. Magical properties: Love, calm, peace, sleep, friendship.

Red clover – use the buds for a purifying and clarifying drink. Magical properties: Luck, money, protection, love, fidelity, exorcism, success.

Rosehips – three or four hips, chopped per cup. Magical properties: Love, psychic powers, healing, luck, protection, peace, mysteries, knowledge, dreams, friendship, death and rebirth, abundance.

Rosemary – a strong flavour, use fresh or dried leaves. Magical properties: Protection, love, lust, mental powers, exorcism, purification, healing, sleep.

Sage – a good stress reliever. Magical properties: Protection, wishes, wisdom, purification, stimulating, intuition, abundance, success.

Sweet violet – six violets per cup. Magical properties: Love, lust, peace, healing, protection, commitment, death and rebirth.

Thyme – good for the digestive system and coughs and colds. Magical properties: Healing, health, peace, psychic powers, love, purification, courage, releasing, sleep, beauty.

And of course, combinations of herbs and plants make good tea blends too. Lemon balm/verbena and ginger work well or lavender and mint. Experiment and see what works for you. If you find herbal teas are not sweet enough for you, add in a teaspoon of honey.

Reminder: If you are pregnant I would recommend avoiding herbal teas unless advised by a qualified professional.

Element garden

Pick one element to work with or section the garden into four and have all of them. Perhaps even in the compass directions they are associated with. Incorporate the colours you associate with the elements and include other items such as pebbles, shells, logs and garden ornaments. Paint representations of the elements onto pots or stones.

Earth could include pebbles, pots and stone statues.

Air lends itself to wind chimes but also bird feeders, bird statues and kites.

Fire most obviously is a fire pit or basket but could also include a barbeque or garden ornaments created from glass.

Water is another easy one in the form of a pond or bird bath but also shells, a water butt or even a watering can. If you don't want a pond you could create a dry river bed using blue glass pebbles or shingle.

Add a small altar or shrine in each section dedicated to the element.

If you have the space to create a small area in the centre of all the elements it would be the perfect place to sit and work with the balance of all the elements, a sweet spot.

You could plant according to colours; the air bed could be yellows, fire might be reds, earth could be green foliage plants and water might be blue. If you include spirit, that might be whites or purples.

Include the triangle element symbols in each area or design your own: Waves for water, flames for fire, clouds for air and leaves for earth perhaps.

Or work the elementals into it. Fairy statues to represent sylphs, lizards for fire, mermaids for water and the good old garden gnome complete with fishing rod for earth – have fun with it.

Earth plants

Beech, cornflower, cramp bark, cypress, dogwood, echinacea, grass, honesty, honeysuckle, horsetail, knotweed, lungwort, magnolia, mugwort, plantain, primrose, sorrel, tulip, valerian, vervain and yew.

Air plants

Agrimony, alyssum, beech, bergamot, birch, borage, bracken, broom, clover, columbine (aquilegia), dandelion, dock, eucalyptus, fern, goldenrod, hazel, horehound, lavender, lemon verbena, lily of the valley, marjoram, meadowsweet, mint, mistletoe, morning glory, parsley, pine and sage.

Fire plants

Anemone, angelica, ash, basil, bay, betony, blackthorn, buttercup, carnation, cedar, celandine, chestnut, chrysanthemum, cleavers, coriander, dill, dittany, fennel, garlic, ginger, gorse, hawthorn, heliotrope, holly, horseradish, hyssop, juniper, lovage, mandrake, marigold, mullein, mustard, nettle, oak, pennyroyal, peony, pine, rosemary, rowan, rue, St John's wort, snapdragon, sunflower, thistle, walnut, witch hazel, woodruff and wormwood.

Water plants

African violet, alexanders, aloe, ash, aster, belladonna, birch, bleeding heart, bluebell, burdock, calamus, camellia, catnip, chamomile, chickweed, columbine (aquilegia), comfrey, cornflower, cowslip, crocus, cyclamen, daffodil, daisy, delphinium, dittany of Crete, elder, eucalyptus, evening primrose, feverfew, foxglove, geranium, gourd, heather, hyacinth, iris, ivy, jasmine, lady's mantle, lemon balm, lilac, lily, lobelia, mallow, myrtle, oak, orchid, pansy, passionflower, periwinkle, poppy, rose, self-heal, skullcap, sea holly, Solomon's seal, sweet pea, tansy, thyme, valerian, violet, willow, yarrow and yew.

Scented garden

This one does what it says on the tin, all the plants are scented. Not just herbs, as lots of flowers have beautiful scents. Roses being perhaps one of the obvious but check before you buy as a lot of modern roses lack any kind of scent.

Scented plants work best when grown in a sheltered area where the fragrance is contained slightly. Place smaller scented plants at the front of raised beds or in containers or wall hangers. Put them where you will brush past them and easily take in the aroma.

Obviously, there are lots of scented plants, some are stronger than others but here are some ideas:

Roses, lavender, honeysuckle, sweet pea, jasmine, acacia, philadelphus, daphne, syringa, choisya, wisteria, magnolia, iberis sempervirens, echinacea, buddleia, viburnum, dianthus, heliotrope, hesperis, lilies, actaea, phlox, nicotiana, clematis montana, nepeta, peony, erysimum, chocolate cosmos, witch hazel, winter sweet, honesty, stocks, rhododendron, chocolate vine and of course most of the herbs.

Scented pelargoniums – these come in all kinds of different varieties with scents such as mint, apple, chocolate and rose but they are not generally hardy.

Gothic garden

All witches love black right? Add in a bit of dark purple and blood red and you are sorted. There are a few true black flowers but not too many, so you may want to add in dark purple as well, it creates a very gothic effect.

Include touches such as wrought iron ornaments, statues, urns, gargoyles and candlesticks with gothic arches and a mirror or two and the stage is set. You could even work in black shingle on the pathways.

Gothic gardens were popular in the Victorian era. Filled with morbid effects and reflections of death, they were real crowd pullers. You could go the whole ten miles and have moss covered tomb stones. Suggested plants for a Gothic garden:

Queen of the Night tulip – spring flowering.

Purple calla lily – symbolises rebirth and resurrection.

Hellebore – usually pink or white there is a really dark purple variety, spring flowering.

Bat orchid – very dark brown that looks black, sometimes called the 'devil flower' or 'cat's whiskers'.

Black pansy – this is a really dark purple that looks black.

Black dahlia – actually a really deep, dark red; it has a mysterious air to it.

Black petunia – we grew these last year and they really do look like black velvet.

Chocolate cosmos – not actually black, these are a dark

brown/burgundy colour, but have the added bonus of a chocolate scent.

Viola 'Molly Sanderson' – these work indoors or outside and grow very well in containers.

Black Baccara rose – a tea rose with very dark burgundy petals.

Physocarpus opulifolius 'Diabolo' sy. 'Monlo' – complicated name but beautiful deep purple/burgundy foliage with small white flowers.

Iris 'before the storm' – a scented purple/black iris.

Cranesbill geranium 'Black Widow' – also called the 'mourning widow', apart from the fabulous name it has pretty crinkled flowers in a dark purple/black with brown splodges on the green leaves.

Chocolate lily (Fritillaria camschatcensis (L.) – despite the name it is not the best scent in the world and has a habit of attracting flies (which pollinate them) this lily has dark brown flowers.

Hollyhock – there are several varieties of dark hollyhocks with brown/purple or near black flowers such as 'Nigra' and 'Black Magic'. Obviously, the latter would be perfect in a witch's garden ...

Elderflower 'Sambucus nigra' comes with purple/black foliage and pale pink flowers.

Black mondo grass – this really looks black and has small white flowers in the summer followed by black seeds. It would not look out of place on a far-off planet in a Star Trek episode.

Aeonium arboretum – a rosette shaped succulent with dark burgundy/brown leaves (this is not hardy).

Canna 'Black Tropicanna' – bright orange flowers supported by dark brown/burgundy foliage (not hardy).

Colocasia 'Black Magic' (there's that name again) – large dark purple/black foliage, this is a dramatic plant but best suited to warm temperatures.

Coleus 'Black Prince' – really easy to grow with striking foliage, usually grown as an annual.

Silver laced primrose – this is so pretty, black petals edge in white with yellow centres.

Heuchera 'Obsidian' – heucheras are one of my favourite foliage plants, this one has deep purple leaves and tiny white/pink flowers.

Phormium/Cordyline – these plants have sword shaped leaves and come in all sorts of colours including dark burgundy.

Purple basil – does what it says on the tin, this is a purple basil.

Black bamboo – the stem/trunk is jet black with green leaves, very striking but bear in mind it can grow very tall.

Tomatoes – if you want to add produce to your Gothic garden there are several garden tomatoes that come in purple.

Swiss chard – purple foliage and of course edible.

Bell/Sweet Pepper 'Purple beauty' – purple peppers!

Aubergine/Eggplant – these are obviously purple.

Corn 'Black Aztec' – corn on the cob in a dark shade.

Blackberries – are of course, black (Okay, maybe they are more purple).

Millet – there are a variety of ornamental grasses that have dark foliage, millet is one of them.

'Dark Angel' Hydrangea has dark foliage with bright purple flowers.

Black ligulana dentata 'Britt Marie Crawford' – dark foliage with contrasting yellow flowers.

Ajuga 'Burgundy Glow' – ground cover with burgundy foliage.

Actea simplex – dark foliage topped with tall pink/white flower spikes in summer.

Acers come in some very dark red and burgundy shades.

Burgundy Lobelia 'Queen Victoria' – we have this in our garden and it is quite stunning, dark burgundy foliage with scarlet flowers.

Burgundy sedum – with dark foliage and pink flowers.

Red knotweed – with burgundy foliage, this is also very hardy.

Alliums come in dark purple shades.

Red castor bean – has large striking purple foliage (poisonous seeds).

Bloodleaf – a filler for borders with dark red/burgundy foliage.

Sweet potato 'Blackie' – an ornamental sweet potato providing deep burgundy leaves with pink flowers in the summer.

Gladioli – these come in shades of burgundy to almost black.

Buddleia – comes in shades of purple and the butterflies love it.

Verbena – provides summer colour and comes in shades of purple.

Lavender – obviously comes in purple!

Clematis – provides climbing height and comes in shades of dark red and deep purple.

Salvia – tall spikes of flowers in purple shades.

Monkshood – fabulous name and comes in purple.

Hyacinth 'Midnight Mystique' – these sweetly scented spring flowers are dark purple.

Elephant Ear Colocasia 'Black Magic' – very dramatic purple foliage plants.

Sweet William 'Sooty' – dark burgundy flower heads.

Rose 'Black Magic' or 'Black Beauty' – not really black at all, in fact not even dark burgundy but they have cool names and come in dark red shades.

Delphinium 'Black Night' – beautiful spikes of dark purple flowers.

Sunflower 'Moulin Rouge' – our well-known sunflowers but

in a shade of dark burgundy/red.

Carnivorous bog garden

A bog garden with carnivorous plants would work well inside a Gothic style garden or used as an indoor garden.

Probably the most well-known carnivorous plant is the Venus flytrap. We had them when we were children and generally killed them by poking the traps too often to watch them close.

There is a vast range of carnivorous plants, a lot of them need to be indoors but some are hardy. They make an interesting indoor garden or an outside bog garden. The common ones:

The Venus flytrap is the Dionaea muscipula species with lots of varieties.

Sundews (Drosera) vary in size and shape and come in nearly 200 varieties. Most have tentacles with sticky ends (perfect for a Steampunk themed garden!).

Butterwords (Pinguicula) sounds like a yummy candy but alas not. About 100 species, they normally have glossy green leaves growing in a rosette. The leaves are sticky.

Pitcher Plants – North American, Tropical, West Australian, Sun and Cobra Lily. Identified because they look like pitchers.

Bladderwarts (Utricularia) – over 200 species, they capture their prey with bladder like organs on their roots which are under water ... creepy.

These plants like sunlight and water. They are bog plants, so they need moist soil. Do your research as they are a bit particular about soil types. They also prefer pure water such as rain or distilled water. They really don't like tap water.

Wildlife garden

Encourage the wildlife into your garden. Birds can be enticed in by adding bird boxes, feeders and a bird bath. They also love hedges, trees and bushes with somewhere safe to perch. Adjust the bird food you put out to attract diverse types of birds; they all have their own particular likes and dislikes (it is like feeding fussy children). The birds in return will help by eating pests and may even gift you with a feather or two.

Trees are not only loved by birds but also provide food for foxes, badgers and deer. Hedgerows provide cover and corridors for small animals.

Long grass provides places for egg laying insects such as butterflies.

I love bats and when we stayed in France a few years ago we would sit outside at dusk and watch the baby bats zipping about like mad above our heads, it was amazing. Fix up a bat box to offer housing to our nighttime friends. The added bonus is they like to eat insects. Night scented plants are good for moths and in turn, bats.

Quite often when clearing away leaves in a corner of our garden I have been surprised by a toad jumping out. They like damp and shady areas.

And of course, a pond provides home to a wide variety of wildlife such as fish (obviously), frogs, insects and the beautiful dragonfly.

Hedgehogs like a cosy place to hibernate and you can make or buy little hedgehog houses for them, they also need space under fences to get in and out of your garden. NEVER leave out milk and/or bread for hedgehogs; it is really bad for them. If you want to leave food, put out a dish of water and one containing dog food. Always check any piles of leaves or grass cuttings before moving in case a hog has decided to hibernate there.

'Insect hotels' is the posh and trendy name for a small space or frame filled with natural items such as logs and hollow stems for bees and insects to make their home in.

If you can, leave an area of your garden uncultivated or plant a wildflower area.

Choose plants that flower for a long season. Plants that have berries are good too. Try to limit highly bred cultivars that contain little or no pollen.

Grow a mixture of plants, flowers, trees and shrubs.

Plants that wildlife particularly love:

Sunflower, foxglove, thyme, lavender, honeysuckle, rowan, sedum, pyracantha, berberis, purple loosestrife, bramble, buddleia, cotoneaster, crab apple, daisies, dandelions, thistle, dogwood, viburnum, hawthorn, holly, ivy and roses.

If you want to be specific:

For the bees:

Fruit trees, crab apple, black/red currants, gooseberries, alyssum, aquilegia, berberis, crocus, forget me not, hawthorn, holly, honesty, beans, allium, borage, campanula, chives, cornflower, fennel, foxglove, geranium, hebe, heliotrope, lavender, lupin, monarda, monkshood, rose, verbena, sage, rosemary, thyme, oregano, eryngium, hollyhock, ivy, mallow, honeysuckle, scabious, aster, buddleia, catmint, dahlia, echinacea, sedum, sunflower, teasel, pyracantha, pulmonaria, heather, rowan, snowdrop and wisteria.

For the butterflies:

Alyssum, aubrietia, forget me not, hawthorn, holly, honesty, pyracantha, wallflower, allium, chives, cornflower, fennel, hebe, heliotrope, lavender, marigold, phlox, Sweet William, verbena, thyme, oregano, aster, buddleia, catmint, dahlia, echinacea, hebe, ivy, scabious, sedum, sunflower and teasel.

For the birds:

Crab apple, berberis, hawthorn, holy, pyracantha, rowan, cornflower, rose, grasses, echinacea, ivy, honeysuckle, sunflower and teasel.

Herb garden

Herbs can be easily grown from seed or small plants and they don't take long to grow. Plant them in pots, hanging baskets, window boxes or in the borders. Creeping herbs such as thyme work well in between paving and cracks in the wall. If you want to go big then an herb wheel or spiral looks fantastic.

You will have to tailor your herb garden to the type of soil and climate you live in, but tender herbs can be grown in pots as annuals or taken in for the winter.

Remember that a lot of herbs come from Mediterranean climates, so they like well-drained soil. Herbs also grow well without any extra compost of feed although if they are in containers I would feed them occasionally. Most of them need a lot of sunlight so avoid putting them in shady areas. Although parsley, meadowsweet, mint, lemon balm and chives will tolerate some shade and even living in damper soil.

Check whether your chosen herbs are annuals, biennial or perennial. Herbs such as basil, coriander, parsley and dill are fast growing and are usually treated as annuals, so you may need to plant several of each at intervals to ensure a continuous supply throughout the summer. Perennials such as chives, rosemary, sage, thyme, mint and oregano are slower growing, so think about where you want to plant them permanently.

A lot of the herbs are also really easy to grow from seed, particularly the annual ones such as parsley, coriander, dill and basil.

With herbs such as bay, chives, lemon balm, mint, rosemary, sage and thyme you will need to harvest them often; the more you pick the more they will grow. Here are some of the main herbs and their magical properties:

Basil – Wealth, money, prosperity, love, exorcism, protection, happiness, peace.

Bay – Protection, purification, strength, power, healing, creativity, spirituality, psychic powers.

Borage – Psychic powers, courage, protection, happiness, peace.

Chamomile – Sleep, dreams, love, calm, money, relaxation, purification, balancing.

Chives – Exorcism, negative energy, bad habits, protection.

Coriander – Health, healing, peace, love, release, wealth, protection, negativity.

Dill – Protection, love, lust, money, jealousy, balance, clarity, knowledge, magic.

Fennel – Healing, purification, protection, courage, confidence, fertility, initiation.

Fenugreek – Prosperity, blessings, money, nightmares, psychic protection, meditation.

Hyssop – Purification, protection, healing.

Lemon balm – Success, healing, anti-depression, memory, love, anxiety.

Lovage – Protection, love.

Marjoram/Oregano – Love, happiness, health, protection, marriage, grief.

Meadowsweet – Peace, happiness, love.

Mint – Money, healing, exorcism, protection, cleansing, calming.

Parsley – Protection, purification, lust, happiness, fertility, spirit work.

Rosemary – Protection, love, lust, mental powers, exorcism, purification, healing, sleep.

Sage – Protection, wishes, wisdom, purification, stimulating, intuition, abundance, success.

Thyme – Healing, health, peace, psychic powers, love, purification, courage, releasing, sleep, beauty.

Deity garden

A garden design can be used to honour a specific deity or pantheon or even a mixture of gods (as long as they tolerate being next to each other). If you choose an individual deity, select plants that are dedicated or correspond to them. Include a statue or items in the design that relate to them and their characteristics.

I have a large goddess outline painted on the back wall of my garden with a spiral in her centre. I painted it with standard masonry paint. My garden also has large flat stones, pebbles and shells all in honour of the goddess The Cailleach.

Choosing a pantheon theme gives you a structure to work from. Celtic (albeit a loose term) would give you the choice of plants from around the United Kingdom. Roman would take from Italian plants and Greek from plants native to Greece, you get the idea.

If you don't want to focus on just a goddess or god you could have a balanced garden, half dedicated to a god and the other to the goddess.

If you work with a particular god or goddess you will know what plants they like (or suggest to you). If you are thinking of dedicating your garden or a part of it to your deity you may want to sit and meditate to connect with them and ask for inspiration and suggestions. I have found that the gods do have very specific likes and dislikes.

There are lists on the internet and in books that will recommend correspondences; here are some to get you started:

Adonis – anemone, adonis, acacia, bay, lily, narcissus, rose, snowdrop and vine.

Aphrodite – wood anemone, apple, cypress, rose, jasmine,

lily and hyacinth.

Apollo – apple, bay, poplar, mistletoe and orange.

Artemis – amaranth, palm, cypress and asphodel.

Bast – catnip, rue, valerian and vervain.

Brighid – blackberry, angelica, bay, cypress, daffodil, dandelion, fennel, lavender, mugwort, rosemary and snowdrop.

Freya – cowslip, strawberry, elder, birch, cowslip, daisy, primrose and rose.

Hecate – belladonna, cyclamen, cypress, garlic, mandrake, azalea, lavender, dandelion, monkshood, wolfbane, hemlock and mint.

Thor – ash, birch, oak, fern and rose.

Venus – anemone, angelica, apple, apricot and aster.

Vishnu – basil, chamomile, cherry, ginger, hazel, jasmine, lavender, oak, mint, periwinkle, rosemary, sage, St John's wort, sweet pea, verbena and violet.

Zeus – apple, almond, artichoke, cinquefoil and sage.

You can expand your range of plants by focusing on the main characteristics of your deity. For instance, Venus is a god of love so you could create your garden with plants that represent love to you such as roses or a garden in shades of pink, white and red.

If you want to keep with an earthy god, certain deities are associated with gardening (or at a stretch earth, fertility, agriculture and harvest):

Cerridwen, Brigit, Dagda, Cernunnos, Epona, Lugh, Bel, the Horned God, Nuada, Demeter, Persephone, Hecate, Gaea, Cronus, Pan, Adonis, Hades, Druantia, Artemis, Aphrodite, Athena, Mab, Astarte, Hermes, Ceres, Ops, Proserpina, Flora, Saturn, Faunus, Mars, Jupiter, Osiris, Ra, Hapi, Amen, Xochipilli, Seb, Inanna, Isis, Cybele, Tezcatlipoca and Zeus.

Pantheon garden

If you work with deities from a specific pantheon then you may want to theme your garden using plants from the country they come from. Do some research as not everything will grow everywhere. Add in statues and plaques that represent the country and you could create an impressive scene.

Greek plants:

Aconite, almond, anemone, poppy, apple, ash, asphodel, barley, broad bean, prickly ivy, cedar, juniper, wild celery, parsley, chaste tree, cherry, sweet chestnut, crocus, cypress, daffodil, elm, strawflower, fennel, fig, Grecian fir, frankincense tree, grape vine, hazelnut, heliotrope, hellebore, hemlock, hyacinth, iris, ivy, larkspur, bay/laurel, prickly lettuce, Madonna lily, linden, lotus tree, mint, mulberry, mushroom, myrtle, polyanthus, oak, olive, date palm, pear, parsley, pine, pomegranate, poplar, reed, rock rose, strawberry tree, violet, walnut, wheat, willow, wolfsbane and yew.

Celtic plants:

Bilberry, burdock, nettle, mistletoe, dandelion, willow, comfrey, lichen, moss, liverwort, oak, ash, apple, hazel, alder, elder, yew, flax, blackthorn, broom, catnip, eyebright, fern, fir, foxglove, gorse, hawthorn, heather, holly, hops, ivy, meadowsweet, mint, mushroom, mugwort, vervain, pimpernel, fern, betony, mandrake, yarrow, valerian, primrose, garlic, agrimony, apple and juniper.

Egyptian plants:

Lotus, papyrus, palm, wheat, barley, figs, rose, jasmine, anemone, daisy, chrysanthemum, mandrake, poppy, tamarisk, date, pomegranate, olive, peach, grapes, plus, acacia, grasses, bamboo, juniper, narcissus, cornflower, myrtle, celosia, ivy, heliotrope, crinum, dragonwort, lychnis and marjoram.

Norse plants:

Sage, coriander, celery, poppy, henbane, common butterbur, hops, apple, damson, cherry, bishop's weed, dill, vervain, kale, mustard, elder, hazel, parsley, rue, bramble, raspberry, dewberry, strawberry, rose, rowan, hawthorn, angelica, chicory and soapwort.

Chinese plants:

Achillea, acorus, adiantum, alpine pumila, amorphophallus, angelica, aquilegia, arachniodes, arisaema, as arum, aspidistra, astilbe, athyrium, bamboo, begonia, bletilla, borinda bolilana, carex, cimicifuga japonica, colocasia, conigramme japonica, cynanchum ascyrifolium, cypripedium, disporopsis, dryopteris, edgeworthia chrysantha, epimedium, farfugium, fargesia robusta, gymnaster savatieri, hemerocallis, hibiscus, hosta, indigofera, iris, jasmine, juniper, lepisorus, liguaria japonica, liriope, lycoris, lysimachia, milettia puchra, mukdenia rossii, musa basjoo, musella lasiocarpa, oleander, peony, pine, plum blossom, podophyllum, polygonatum, rhododendron, saccharum arundinaceum, saruma henryi, schefflera delavayi, sedum, selaginella, trachelospermum, trachycarpus, yushania confuse, yew and zingiber.

Fiction garden

Theme a garden to your favourite book, it could be Lord of the Rings with plants from the Shire or madness and mayhem in the form of an Alice in Wonderland plot. It might be that you use plants that are mentioned within the pages of the story or find plants that remind you of the tale or the characters.

Alice in Wonderland

You could plant up old teapots and cups with small plants, have twisting pathways, checkerboard stepping stones, tiny doors, tree stumps and archways along with mirrors of course. Ornamental toadstools, rabbits, caterpillars, clocks and pink flamingo statues will all fit in. Go bright with your colours, big with the flowers and bold with the shapes. Alice in wonderland plant suggestions:

Tiger-lily, rose, daisy, violet, larkspur, iris, pansy, tulip, sweet peas, blue bonnets, calla lily, lily of the valley, lilac, sunflower, chrysanthemum, morning glory, daffodil, dandelion, hibiscus, dahlia, clematis, passion flower, allium, fritillaria and thistles.

Hobbit garden
Think Bilbo, Frodo and Sam – a small wooden doorway in the side of a hill with a pretty cottage front garden and a backyard full of vegetables and fruit. Use bright but simple cottage garden style flowers. Maybe a picket fence with a wooden gate and plenty of tree stumps to sit and have a second breakfast whilst enjoying the view. A fruit tree is a must and if there is room for a little hobbit shed that would be perfect. Add a log pile and a little homemade stream to finish it off. Hobbit plant suggestions:

Nasturtiums, snapdragon, sunflower, sweet pea, pansy, geranium/pelargonium, cornflower, poppy, petunia, crocus, roses, marigold, foxglove and iris. Apple, plum, cherry, cauliflower, celery, garlic, carrot, pea, potato, cabbage, lettuce, tomato, sweetcorn, turnip and strawberry. Angelica, basil, dill, lavender, lemon balm, marjoram, mint, rosemary, tarragon and parsley.

Harry Potter garden
If you want your land to look like part of the wizarding world you could add a bit of Potter magic. Pebbles (philosopher's

stone), cauldrons filled with plants, owl statues, besoms and twigs (broomsticks) and maybe signs directing people to Hagrid's Hut or keeping them out of the forbidden forest. Look through the Doctrine of Signatures for ideas on some plants to use. Harry Potter plant suggestions:

Mandrake, cactus, carnivorous plants, wolfsbane, lavender, belladonna, dittany, willow, asphodel, holly, elder, rowan, yew, hawthorn, ash, aconite, agapanthus, aloe vera, angel's trumpet, arnica, ginger, hellebore, hemlock, henbane, hydrangea, sage, rue, begonia, betony, borage, lady's mantle, lily, lovage, St John's wort, thistle, thyme, cornflower, mistletoe, mint, valerian, nasturtium, nettle, nightshade, dandelion, valerian, peony, foxglove, rhododendron and roses.

Wildflower garden

Go wild!

Wildflower gardens or patches of wildflower meadows in a garden look fabulous and the wildlife love them. You can actually purchase wildflower mead turf to lay in your garden, which does sound a bit mad. The turf is already implanted with wildflower plants and seeds. But a cheaper option is to buy seed and you can get very good wild flower mixes. Alternatively collect seeds from the wild but be careful to identify the species correctly and don't trespass.

This is a very low maintenance garden as it is left alone most of the year and just needs mowing in the autumn. It is essentially an organised chaos garden.

Expanding on the wild flower garden, you could include lots of wild plants for foraging; the type of plants you find when you venture out into the woods and hedgerows. Things such as hawthorn, wild garlic and elderflower but also lots of edible weeds.

Ensure the seed mix is compatible with your soil type. In you are including grasses in your mix make sure you have more flowers to grass ratio as grasses can be bullies. Introducing 'yellow rattle' in your mix can help as this plant keeps other grasses in check.

Sow in the spring or autumn but be patient, it may take a couple of years to really come into its own. And each year it will self-seed and produce more wonderful flowers. Suggestions for a wildflower garden:

Cowslip, birdsfoot trefoil, lady's bedstraw, rough hawskbit, red clover, ox eye daisy, yellow rattle, meadow buttercup, selfheal, sorrel, tufted vetch, knapweed, toadflax, musk mallow, ragged robin, cornflowers, poppies, bladder campion, bluebell, common vetch, creeping buttercup, cow parsley, garlic mustard, greater celandine, hedge bedstraw, meadow cranesbill, red campion, rib worth plantain, white deadnettle, hedge parsley, wood owens, yarrow, yellow meadow vetch, common bent, slender creeping red fescue, meadow grass and tufted hair grass.

Note if collecting seed from the wild: Ethical wildcrafting is the practice of harvesting plants and trees conscientiously, to avoid damaging the health of the population or the overall ecological system. With seeds and fruits maybe just make sure you ask the plant first if it is Okay for you to harvest the fruits and leave an offering in place and please don't take more than you need. Leave enough for others, for animals and birds and in the case of seeds, for the plant to reseed itself. Make sure to only take a small amount and leave enough of the plant in situ so that it can continue to grow. Please also note that some plants in the wild are protected and even on the verge of extinction.

Fairy garden

Fairy gardens do seem to be extremely popular and can look incredibly effective. I would use caution here, inviting the fair folk into your garden can seem like a lovely idea but please, I urge you to do some proper research first (I recommend reading the works of author Morgan Daimler).

Working with the world of fairy is not for the faint hearted, nor is it all gossamer wings and sparkly glitter. We have the Victorians' ideas of fancy to thank for the twee vision of fluttery flower fairies. Fairies need to be dealt with respectfully (but thank them with gifts as the words 'thank you' are irrelevant to them). There is a whole encyclopaedia of fairy etiquette which needs to be followed. I don't want to put you off because working with the fae can be rewarding, just make sure you have done some proper research about their likes, dislikes and how to treat them first.

Essentially you are dealing with a different realm, the fae do not think or act necessarily as we do or how you might expect them to. Some fae are friendly and helpful, some like to cause chaos and mayhem and others are just plain unfriendly, approach with caution, research and be prepared.

You can find an immense variety of fairy statues in the garden centres. Use pebbles and water features, hang mirrors and sparkly beads and lights in the trees. The fae do seem to like things that shimmer and shine. Give them some dark shady areas too. Fairies do love gardens, flowers, trees and plants and there are some that they seem to be drawn to more than others such as:

Apple, ash, bay, bean, betony, birch, bracken, bramble, celandine, chicory, clover, columbine (aquilegia), cornflower, cowslip, cyclamen, daisy, delphinium, elder, evening primrose, fern, foxglove, hawthorn, hazel, heather, hemp, henbane, honesty, honeysuckle, lavender, lilac, lily of the valley, mandrake, meadowsweet, morning glory, nightshade, oak, periwinkle, primrose, rose, rosemary, rowan, rue, snapdragon, snowdrop, thorn, thyme, wild rose, valerian, vervain and yarrow.

Planetary garden

I have covered sun and moon themed gardens but what about a garden dedicated to the planets? Section your garden into eight to represent Mercury, Venus, Mars, Jupiter, Saturn, Uranus, Neptune and Pluto. Or make it ten and include the Sun and the Moon as well. Pick colours that you think represent each planet or use plants that are associated with each one.

Jupiter

Agrimony, betony, birch, borage, cedar, chestnut, cinquefoil, dandelion, dock, honeysuckle, hyssop, juniper, meadowsweet, oak, sage, thistle and valerian.

Mars

Anemone, basil, belladonna, blackthorn, broom, coriander, echinacea, garlic, ginger, gorse, hawthorn, holly, horseradish, mustard, nettle, oak, pennyroyal, pine, poppy, rue, snapdragon, thistle, woodruff and wormwood.

Mercury

Bergamot, bluebell, bracken, cinquefoil, clover, dill, elm, fennel, fern, horehound, lavender, lemon verbena, lily of the valley, lungwort, mandrake, marjoram, mint, mullein, parsley, rowan, sweet pea and yew.

Moon

Aloe, birch, calamus, camellia, chickweed, dittany, eucalyptus, evening primrose, gourd, honesty, hyssop, iris, ivy, jasmine, juniper, lemon balm, lily, mallow, mugwort, myrtle, poppy, rose, sweet pea, willow and wormwood.

Neptune

Ash, night blooming jasmine, lobelia, morning glory, pine, reed, water lily and white mulberry.

Saturn

Aloe, beech, belladonna, blackthorn, cleavers, comfrey, cornflower, cypress, datura, elm, foxglove, holly, horsetail, ivy, knotweed, lobelia, mullein, pansy, pine, skullcap, Solomon's seal, witch hazel and yew.

Sun

Angelica, ash, bay, bergamot, buttercup, calamus, carnation, cedar, celandine, chamomile, chrysanthemum, eucalyptus, hazel, heliotrope, juniper, lovage, marigold, mistletoe, morning glory, oak, peony, rosemary, rowan, rue, St John's wort, sunflower, walnut and witch hazel.

Venus

African violet, angelica, aster, birch, bleeding heart, burdock, catnip, coltsfoot, columbine (aquilegia), cornflower, cowslip, crocus, cyclamen, daffodil, daisy, datura, delphinium, dittany of Crete, echinacea, elder, feverfew, foxglove, geranium, goldenrod, hawthorn, heather, hyacinth, iris, jasmine, lady's mantle, lemon balm, lilac, lily, magnolia, mallow, mint, mugwort, myrtle, orchid, pansy, passionflower, pennyroyal, periwinkle, plantain, poppy, primrose, rose, self-heal, sea holly, sorrel, sweet pea, tansy, thyme, tulip, valerian, vervain, violet and yarrow.

Zodiac garden

If working with sun signs is your thing, you could theme your garden to your own personal zodiac sign or section it into twelve and include all of them:

Aries

Bay, clover, coriander, cowslip, feverfew, garlic, ginger, horseradish, juniper, marjoram, mustard, nettle and rosemary.

Aquarius

Bergamot, borage, crocus, cypress, elder, fennel, iris, mint, mullein and St John's wort.

Cancer

Agrimony, angelica, catnip, daisy, dill, honeysuckle, hyssop, jasmine, lemon balm, mandrake, mint, mugwort, violet and wormwood.

Capricorn

Comfrey, buttercup, marjoram, pine, plantain, poppy, Solomon's seal, sorrel and witch hazel.

Gemini

Angelica, bergamot, betony, cinquefoil, dill, honeysuckle, lavender, meadowsweet, mint, parsley, snapdragon, tansy, thyme and vervain.

Leo

Angelica, bay, borage, burdock, chamomile, daffodil, dill, fennel, heliotrope, lavender, marigold, mint, mistletoe, parsley, rue and sunflower.

Libra

Angelica, aster, bergamot, burdock, catnip, elder, feverfew, pennyroyal, Saint John's wort, thyme and violet.

Pisces
Fern, geranium, lemon verbena, lily of the valley, lungwort, meadowsweet, rose and willow.

Sagittarius
Agrimony, aloe, beech, betony, birch, cedar, elder, feverfew, hawthorn, oak, rowan and sage.

Scorpio
Basil, blackthorn, cowslip, horehound, ivy, lady's mantle, lily, nettle, pennyroyal and wormwood.

Taurus
Cinquefoil, coltsfoot, daisy, dandelion, fern, iris, lovage, lungwort, mandrake, mint, myrtle, sage, sorrel and thyme.

Virgo
Bergamot, fennel, mandrake, skullcap and valerian.

Tiny gardens for indoors
If you don't have a garden there is no need to despair, utilise your window sills, tables near windows and bathrooms. Kitchen window sills lend themselves perfectly to pots of herbs which are easy to look after, and bathrooms are perfect for succulents or air plants. Air plants don't even need to be in soil, they get everything they need through their leaves.

Setting out an indoor garden can be just a couple of plants on a window sill or entire windows full of pots and hanging baskets. Plants generally need light, so you will have to use a window sill, or a table/unit pushed up against a window. We have a long table in our conservatory that in the spring is taken over with seed trays.

Of course, the bonus with growing plants indoors is that you don't have to worry about frost. Still be thoughtful about your choices because some plants don't like draughts and others can be temperamental by a radiator.

Mini indoor gardens can challenge your creativity. A large flat dish can be planted with succulents or bottle gardens and terrariums are intriguing to work with, be careful when watering as these often don't have drainage.

You can create your own terrarium garden using any glass container. Add a layer of pebbles on the bottom for drainage, then a layer of activated charcoal followed by a layer of sphagnum moss over the charcoal. Pre-moisten the soil so that it is damp and add a good layer (3 to 4 inches) on top of the moss. If you want larger plants, then add a deeper layer of soil. Then pop your plants in. Finish by covering the container with a lid. It should be kept in a light place but out of direct sunlight. If the soil gets too wet, leave the top off for a while. You could create mini worlds inside using small coloured stones and tiny decorations.

You can perform plant blessings on your indoor garden just as you would outside. Suggested terrarium plants:

Friendship plant, spider fern, peperomia, starfish plant, silver nerve plant, aquamarine, golden clubmoss, spiderwort, African violet, strawberry begonia, artillery fern, aluminium plant, hypoestes, prayer plant, pothos, bloodleaf iresine, button fern, earth star, flame violet, pin cushion plant, arrowhead vine and asparagus fern.

Colour magic

I work with colour magic and that carries on into the world of magical plants and flowers.

Roses especially have magical properties associated with their colours:

Red – passion, love, romance.
Pink – friendship, love.
White – peace, clarity, purity.
Yellow – happiness, friendship.

My own garden has various flower beds, but we stick to colour palettes for each. So, our 'hot bed' has reds, oranges and bright yellows; whereas our 'cool beds' have shades of pink, blue, white and purple.

You can mix it up and left to its own devices nature does just that, but we have found block colours or complementary palettes work extremely well.

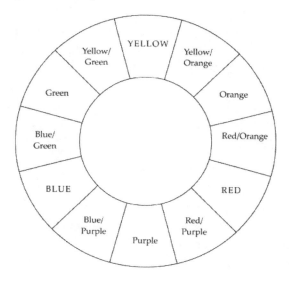

The colour wheel gives you a good starting point. Complementary colours are those directly opposite each other on the wheel. For instance, blue and orange or red and green.

Harmonious colours are those that sit next to each other on the wheel, for example, blue and violet or red and red/orange and orange.

Triadic colours involve drawing an equilateral triangle (might have to dig deep into your school maths lesson memories) on the wheel, the three points indicate the matching colours such as red, blue and yellow.

Monochrome – a garden using the shades of one single colour. An all-white garden can look stunning with the backdrop of green foliage. A blue garden going from palest sky blue through the shades to dark blue can look fantastic. It also helps to narrow down the decisions to be made when in the garden centre of course!

Hot colours such as vibrant reds, oranges and bright yellow give a warm, spicy look to the garden. Over on the dark side blacks, deep blues and purples can create a sultry mysterious feel. On the softer side pale yellow, white and pastel colours can be soothing, calming and relaxing.

Colours of course have magical associations, here is a list to start with but be guided by your own intuition: (List taken from *Grimoire of a Kitchen Witch*.)

Black – protection, ward negativity, remove hexes, spirit contact, truth, remove discord or confusion and binding for spell work.

Dark blue – the Goddess, water elemental, truth, dreams, protection, change, meditation, healing.

Light blue – psychic awareness, intuition, opportunity, understanding, safe journey, patience, tranquillity, ward depression, healing and health.

Brown – endurance, houses and homes, uncertainties,

influence friendships.

Green – earth elemental, nature magic, luck, fertility, healing, balance, courage, work, prosperity, changing directions or attitudes.

Indigo – meditation, spirit communication, karma workings, neutralize baneful magic, ward slander.

Lilac – spiritual development, psychic growth, divination, Otherworld.

Orange – the God, strength, healing, attracting things, vitality, adaptability, luck, encouragement, clearing the mind, justice, career goals, legal matters, selling, action, ambition, general success.

Pink – honour, morality, friendships, emotional love, social ability, good will, caring, healing emotions, peace, affection, nurturing, romance and partnerships.

Purple – power, spirit, spiritual development, intuition, ambition, healing, wisdom, progress, business, spirit communication, protection, occultism, self-assurance.

Red – fire elemental, strength, power, energy, health, vigour, enthusiasm, courage, passion, sexuality, vibrancy, survival, driving force.

White – purity, protection, truth, meditation, peace, sincerity, justice and to ward off doubt and fear.

Yellow – air elemental, divination, clairvoyance, mental alertness, intellect, memory, prosperity, learning, changes, harmony, creativity, self-promotion.

When using pots indoors or out you can add magic by painting them a specific colour and/or drawing symbols on them. For instance, a mint plant in a green pot with a dollar/pound sign drawn on the pot would make an excellent prosperity plant spell.

Crystals in the garden

I have several crystals dotted around the garden, mainly natural quartz. They have been placed where my intuition has guided me to. But you can bury specific crystals beside plants to add to their magical properties. The plants will pick up the energy from the crystal as they grow.

Carry a crystal with you to impart the properties (for instance moss agate will help keep your energy levels up whilst you are gardening). Hang crystals in fruit trees to improve the harvest.

Place crystals around the garden to form a grid or around individual plants in a circle to bring in positive energy and to focus and intensify the energy. Place crystals in a geometric pattern around a small area or the entire garden, the stones can be activated so that the energy flows between the grid.

Bring the elements to your garden in crystal form: Select four crystals that represent the elements, one for each (earth, air, fire and water). Bury each crystal in your garden at the direction for the element it represents (north, east, south and west). As you bury each one you might like to say a chant or a blessing asking for a successful and productive garden.

You can also place crystals under the soil to cleanse and purify them. Leave them there overnight but remember where you buried them! This works especially well with crystals that align with the element of earth.

Crystal water

Crystal water can be easily created and used to water plants that need a boost of energy:

Pop a crystal into distilled water (boiled and cooled water) and leave it in the sun and/or the moon for a day and a night. Leave it in the sun for a shot of male energy or in the moon to soak up her feminine power. You can leave it out in both for a balance of energy. Once charged with the energy from the crystal, you can use it to water your plants. Quartz crystals such as rose, amethyst and citrine work well for this. You can also pop a crystal into your plant feed for a few hours before you use it to soak up a boost of energy from the feed.

If you cut flowers from your garden to put in a vase, drop a crystal into the water to help the flowers last.

Not crystals, but I do have some very pretty coloured glass pebbles/stones sprinkled amongst the gravel on the pathways in my garden. When it rains, or the sun shines it picks up the colours and sparkles which looks really pretty.

I would suggest not placing any expensive crystals outside, the weather will take its toll on them and some of the softer more absorbent ones will deteriorate over time.

Note: There is a bit of a debate about working with crystals because they are removed from Mother Earth through a mining process. You have to make the choice whether you want to work with them or not. You might prefer to seek out crystals that have been ethically and ecologically sourced and not from areas that have been overmined.

The crystals I use in my garden have all be found at charity/ thrift shops and I feel that by returning them to the soil they are thankful and as a response will look after the plants for me. Suggested garden crystals:

Moss agate – this must be an obvious choice from the name and the looks; it absolutely screams 'garden'. Moss agate promotes: Grounding, a connection to nature, gardening skills, plant vitality, abundance, healing and encourages nature spirits.

Moonstone – bringing in the energy of the moon to your garden. A symbol of fertility it promotes growth and a restful feel to the garden.

Moonstone promotes: Moon magic (obviously), rest,

restoration, health and fertility.

Green calcite – any of the green stones seem to promote nature to me but calcite in particular works to bring a calm energy into your outside space. Said to belong to the earth spirits, offer them a small stone with thanks. Pop a piece in your garden to promote a peaceful and calm atmosphere.

Green calcite promotes: Soothing, calming and de-stressing, fertility, encouragement, positive energy, stimulation, transformation and cultivation.

Malachite – another green stone bringing the connection to nature but also abundance. Place in your garden to protect the plants from electromagnetic fields.

Malachite promotes: Fertility, vegetation, growth, abundance, supports the environment and brings protection against EMF.

Clear quartz – my crystal of choice for the garden because it is not only inexpensive but is a good 'all round' crystal. Place a piece beneath the soil and it will work its magic to stimulate growth. Bury clear quartz point upwards in pots and place tumble stones around them.

Clear quartz promotes: Healing, vitality and boosts the energy of other stones.

Tiger's Eye – a beautiful earthy coloured stone.

Tiger's eye promotes: Courage, strength, growth, harmony and wealth.

Citrine – a stone full of sunshine colours but remember the sun will fade this stone quite quickly. Citrine promotes: Cleansing, energy, protection, dispels negative energy, protects the environment and brings abundance.

Rhyolite – for gardens that struggle with challenges this also works well in succulent gardens. Any gardens that present a challenge in growing conditions, location or climate.

Green aventurine – eases stress and cares for the environment.

Aquamarine – if you have a pond or water in your garden,

pop a piece of aquamarine in the water to keep the fish and plants happy.

Cerussite – use in the garden to protect against aphids. Also helps keep house plants healthy.

Daphnite – a stone of transformation, it can encourage growth and abundance for all plants and harvests.

Green tourmaline – a healing stone, it can also bring balance. Use to increase the magical and medicinal properties of all herbs. The spirit of the entire plant kingdom is said to reside within this stone. It helps make the connection between the earth and the plants to help them grow.

Fossils work well in the garden, they not only look beautiful as decorations, but they provide a link to our ancestors and how the soil preserves and encourages life.

Rose quartz is an excellent stone to help roses grow successfully.

Bloodstone is good with honeysuckle.

Use amethyst, fluorite and lepidolite with your herbs especially lavender, sage and basil.

Tiger's eye works well for garlic, lilies, gladioli and pansies.

Citrine and fluorite assist with all citrus fruits.

Carnelian and pyrite help with salads, peppers, tomatoes, nasturtiums and poppies.

Rhodonite is a good crystal to pop beside lettuce, celery and tulips.

For poorly plants, clear quartz, amethyst, rose quartz, aventurine and sodalite are particularly good, but be guided by your intuition and what you believe the plant needs.

If the roots are in trouble push the crystal into the soil, if the stalk or branch is suffering you can tie the crystal to it – wrap it carefully with soft fabric (a piece of old panty hose/tights works well).

Animals in the garden

Once your garden is up and running the wildlife will arrive which is a wonderful thing (yes even the slugs and snails) Take note if you see any animals in particular, they are fascinating to watch but they also carry magic with them.

Ant

For a couple of years running we had an ants nest in the corner of our conservatory. It was horrible to be honest especially when the flying ant season came around. However, the humble ant plays a big part in the eco system and carries incredible magical energy. Think about a nest full of ants ... industrious just doesn't cover it, these little guys work their butts off. They are also part of a community and work together as a team each one knowing exactly what it needs to do. They also have enormous amounts of patience and determination. They bring honour and respect with them and work together for the good of their community. They also create and design, sometimes huge constructs.

Keywords: Hard work, team work, patience, determination, creating your dreams, community and equality.

Bat

A creature of the night, thanks to Hollywood these 'lil guys have a bit of a spooky reputation. And no, they won't fly into your hair; they have a clever radar satnav on board. Some folklore stories suggest that bats were thought to be witches and if one flew close by you it was a witch checking up on you or sending a curse. They are in fact beautiful highly sensitive creatures who bring intuition, dreams and visions. They also have really cool night vision which can help you to see through illusions and find the truth. The bat is very sociable and loves nothing more than a good ole chat with the rest of the group. Living in the dark caves of Mother Earth, the bat brings rebirth as it emerges from the depths every night. Bat does, however, require a lot of commitment from you so be warned it doesn't work with slackers!

Keywords: Commitment, challenges, renewal, rebirth, communication, intuition, sensitivity, illusion, truth and dreams.

Bee

VERY important to the eco system and our entire existence on this planet. I do all I can to encourage and support them in my garden. Without these little critters whizzing about in their stripy pyjamas we would have no food ... they are incredibly important. They are a representation of birth, death and rebirth and have been worshipped and honoured in many cultures for thousands of years. Often mentioned in myths and folklore is the belief that bees are the souls of those who were worthy to come back to earth. Bees should also be told all the local gossip especially regarding births, deaths and wedding plans ... they need to know this stuff. Bees remind us to take the good stuff from life and to literally make hay (or honey) while the sun shines. Bee tells us to follow our dreams but also with a reminder to plan and save for the future too.

Keywords: Prosperity, good fortune, communication, gossip, reincarnation, goals, celebration, community, achieving your dreams, productivity, co-operation and focus.

Beetle

I am absolutely sure you wouldn't intentionally squish a beetle but folklore states that a whole week of rain will follow if you do ...

Beetles come in all shapes and sizes (like humans really) and bring transformation, metamorphosis and rebirth of ideas, thoughts, spirituality and complete lives. Beetles work in harmony with their surroundings and can teach us to do the same, throwing in the ability to use our intuition too. Beetles are also persistent and strong.

Keywords: Transformation, rebirth, spirituality, harmony, intuition, strength and persistence.

Blackbird

The blackbird sings a very sweet song and it is for this that it is probably most well known in myths and folklore. The song can expand our conscious, heal and take us on spiritua_ and magical journeys. Blackbird has often been seen as a gatekeeper to the Otherworld and realms of Fairy. The blackbird has also long been associated with blacksmiths and blacksmith gods who carry their own very special type of magic as the master of all four elements.

Keywords: Song, communication, healing, spirituality, Otherworld, Fairy, elemental magic, meditation and potential.

Butterfly

The butterfly must be one of the creatures most associated with transformation and change as it emerges from a cocoon into a beautiful winged creature. Just watching a butterfly flit about the garden brings joy and a sense of freedom and happiness. Their bizarre multifaceted eyes allow them to see images incredibly clearly and they can pick up on ultraviolet wavelengths of light, so they have the magic of psychic abilities pretty much built in. Look at the butterfly and how it transforms then watch as it makes the most of life by surrounding itself with colour and nature.

Keywords: Transformation, psychic abilities, changes, beauty, nature, learning, renewal, understanding, happiness and inspiration.

Crow

This is one very powerful animal spirit guide and a clever beggar as well. Crow brings wisdom, knowledge and magic from every dimension and helps us to learn to trust our own intuition. He is also mindful, not just of our own self but also in judging others' actions and words. Crow is very much an eccentric individual and he encourages that in those he chooses to walk with. Crow also brings change, creation, spiritual strength and the ability to see into the past and the future. He is a bit of a cheeky sly one though and deception is not beneath him, in fact sometimes he revels in it. He does teach us to adapt, to look beyond the ordinary and to listen to what is going on around us.

Keywords: Mindfulness, truth, trust, intuition, integrity, individuality, change, past/present/future, spiritual strength, magic, wisdom, deception and awareness.

Dragonfly

Flitting in and out of reeds and water plants, the dragonfly is a master of flight who reflects light and colour. This is one magical and mystical creature that is often associated with the world of Fairy. Dragonfly brings illusion, shapeshifting, changes, transformation, emotions and compassion along with wingfuls of healing energy. Dragonfly helps us to see beyond the normal and the reality into other realms to unleash possibility and changes within ourselves and the magic that the world has to offer us.

Keywords: Magic, mystery, illusion, shapeshifting, change, transformation, emotions, compassion, healing, possibilities and enlightenment.

Fox

The wily cunning ole fox has appeared in myths and legends for centuries bringing his shapeshifting and healing abilities with him. He is skilful, creative and full of the mystical dawn/dusk in between magic that is also often associated with the world of Fairy. He can teach us his cunning and clever ways using camouflage, agility and the art of shapeshifting. He doesn't outrun ... he observes, plans, plots and schemes, anticipating the next move and outwitting those that chase him. He is smart and crafty, but he does go over the top sometimes and becomes unbearably so.

Keywords: Cunning, stealth, courage, observation, persistence, wisdom, magic, shapeshifting and invisibility.

Frog/Toad

We often get a toad in the garden, in fact he likes to scare the living daylights out of me hiding in the dark corners and leaping out when I least suspect it. It was once believed that toads were witches who had shape shifted ... seriously if I was going to shape shift it wouldn't be into a toad ... but it does mean that toad brings cauldrons full of magic and witchcraft with it. Both creatures have very similar magical properties; the frog is just slightly damper. They are a representation of rebirth and new life and a symbol of awakening ... have you kissed any frogs lately? Patience is definitely one of the virtues frog brings as they spend hours sitting still waiting for their prey. The tadpole into frog scenario also creates the powers of transformation and water brings emotions and intuition.

Keywords: Magic, witchcraft, rebirth, new life, awakening, patience, transformation, emotions and intuition.

Grasshopper

The grasshopper sings with its body parts (but apparently generally only the male of the species) and can leap over huge obstacles or into other dimensions, now that's something not everyone can claim to do. They are also ancient and have a very strong medicine connection to the ancestors. Grasshopper also brings good luck and abundance but also offers up opportunities for you to just leap right into, asking you to trust and not always to look before you leap. Jump forwards ... never back.

Keywords: Astral travel, overcoming obstacles, change, ancestors, luck, abundance, opportunity and looking forward.

Hedgehog

Often associated with the world of Fairy, in fact sometimes suggested that the hedgehog is a fairy or even a witch in disguise. Linked with witchcraft the hedgehog has good and bad folklore superstitions. Hedgehogs are mostly active at dawn and dusk, the in between times so they have links to the Otherworld, prophecy and psychic abilities. The hedgehog is probably best known for its defence mechanism of rolling into a ball to present its sharp spines to the world, keeping it safe from predators, reflecting the ability to deal with challenges calmly and effectively. Definitely an earth element creature, the hedgehog brings a huge pack of earth magic along with abundance and fertility.

Keywords: Fairy, witchcraft, psychic abilities, prophecy, Otherworld, defence, challenges, calm, earth magic, abundance and fertility.

Ladybird/ladybug

Called a ladybird in the UK and ladybug in the USA, this tiny little pretty coloured insect is a powerful animal spirit guide. The shell keeps it protected, the wings allow it to fly and they have amazing instincts. Feeling vibrations through their legs to allow them to sense the energy of whatever they are touching. Their bright colours also serve as a warning to predators to keep away, guiding us to send out the same message to our enemies. The colours of this little bug also bring happiness and joy and remind us to let go of fears and live life to the fullest. The ladybird asks us to trust and have faith, not just in ourselves but in those around us to. Ladybird also brings a connection to our past lives, death and rebirth, renewal and spiritual enlightenment.

Keywords: Trust, faith, wishes, luck, protection, happiness, intuition, defence, past lives, cycle of life and enlightenment.

Magpie

This black and white mystical bird brings feathers full of occult knowledge. The magpie is also known as Jack of all trades ... but master of none – dabbling into everything. It is a reminder that whatever task you take on, do it properly and follow it through to completion. Magpie has the ability to open a gateway to the world of spirit and the fairy realms; he can also help with past life exploration. Be warned though ... messing with magic can have consequences and magpie medicine has a tendency to be unpredictable. Magpie is also very vocal (they sit in my garden and shout if there is no food about). Magpie also loves shiny things, which is a warning not to fall prey to the lure of too many material things in life. If you are gifted a feather it carries the magic of magpie with it and can be used in workings.

Keywords: Occult, magic, knowledge, dedication, spirit world, faerie, past life, consequences, communication, clarity, opportunistic, perception, illusion and expression.

Mole

A big part of mole medicine is the ability to trust your senses and instincts and to be able to 'feel' the truth or a lie. Mole lives under the ground so makes an excellent guide to the Underworld and to mysteries and secrets. Mole has faith and can guide you on your spiritual journey.

Keywords: Trust, senses, instincts, truth, guidance, Underworld, mysteries, faith and spirituality.

Rabbit/Hare

Rabbits and hares like to make lots of baby rabbits and hares ... so, fertility is key here. They also have a strong connection to the seasons and the moon. They like to live in burrows, which also gives them an earthy grounded energy. Rabbits and hares are both nocturnal linking them to intuition, emotions and reflection. They are very sociable animals and love a bit of a rabbit get together, but they can also show aggression and jealousy when provoked – much the same as any family or community. They are alert and sensitive to the environment around them and very cautious, but they also like to have a good hop and a skip.

Keywords: Fertility, seasons, moon magic, earth energy, intuition, emotions, reflection, social, community, jealousy, sensitivity, caution and joy.

Robin

Tiny birds … big medicine. A bird of sacrifice and rebirth it also brings happiness, wisdom, change, growth and renewal. The robin is a very caring and nurturing parent. Robin helps you to let go of the past and come out renewed and refreshed. Robin is very territorial, creative and a guide to trusting your intuition. Let go of any dramas or issues and learn to sing a happy robin song.

Keywords: Happiness, guidance, change, growth, renewal, wisdom, nurturing, creativity and intuition.

Spiders

I know, I know … they can be a bit scary. Although if these eight-legged web weavers freak you out it might be worth doing some searching into why. If they are your shadow animal there will be a reason. They don't particularly bother me until I walk into a web at face height … ewwww! Really, they are incredibly magical and have a lot to teach us. They weave the web of fate and bring balance between the past and future bringing spirituality and creativity. Spider brings awareness of your own web of life and how you create and design everything that happens around you. Spider hands back the responsibility of creating your own environment to you, with a reminder that YOU are in charge. Spider webs can be used in magic to symbolise the web of life that you wish to create for yourself.

Keywords: Creation, weaving reality, infinity, balance, past/present/future, responsibility and spirituality.

Slugs and snails

We do suffer with these in our garden and they can do a lot of damage to the plants. Whole trays of marigolds have disappeared overnight to be left as mere stalks due to these little blighters. However, they do have their place in the whole scheme of things and magic in abundance.

Okay, so it probably wouldn't be your first choice for an animal spirit guide but if it comes your way don't argue ... go with it, there will be a reason. One of the main purposes for snail's arrival is to bring you patience by the slime load. Snail knows that good things come to those who wait and anything important is worth doing properly and at a steady pace. Life is all too fast, and we should all slow down and give ourselves time to smell the roses. Snails are generally quite small, so it also brings the message that you might need to focus on the detail and take notice of the smaller things. And of course, the snail is protected by an outer shell, so it brings protective qualities as well as the idea that sometimes you need to withdraw and have some 'me time'. If you find any empty snail shells in your garden (if the blackbirds have had a snack) you can use them in magical workings to represent the magic snail brings with it.

Keywords: Patience, protection, spiral of life, letting go of deadlines, slowing down, paying attention to details, inner work and withdrawal.

Wasps

Possibly one of the only insects I really dislike, although we don't seem to have had so many around in the last few years. He is apparently revered in quite a few cultures being a symbol of evolution, creator, organiser and keeping control over life situations. He is also a pollinator so don't discount his magic for fertility and productivity. He is also quite social (and not just when he is after your pint of beer), so he brings the magic of communication and the ability to express himself.

Shameless plug: If you want to work more with the animals you see in your garden, check out my book *Pagan Portals Animal Magic* to learn about animal spirit guides.

Poorly plants, pests and disease

No matter how experienced you are as a gardener, on occasion you will get poorly plants. Your first step is to make sure it doesn't have an aphid or fungal problem. Then check to make sure it is in the right soil or light/shade conditions. Make any treatments that are necessary, but you can also add a little healing magic.

If the plant is in a pot you could move it to your altar area for a while. We have an alley way at the end of our garden that we refer to as 'the hospital wing'. If a plant is suffering we pop it in the alleyway and leave it alone for a while. Somehow, magically, when we go back a few weeks later the plant has usually recovered.

If the plant is in the ground you could send healing energy, use visualisation to 'see' the plant recovering, and you can also add healing crystals around it. It may also be worth asking the plant what the issue is.

Our gardens are part of a much larger eco system and will become home to a wide variety of wildlife. Some unfortunately can do a lot of damage to the plants. Disease can also attack and whilst some can be ignored, others will decimate a plant. The choice on whether to take action or what actions to take is yours to make. Obviously, there are chemical pesticides and fungicides but do consider the damage they do to the natural balance in your garden.

A lot of the insects that damage plants can be picked off, if you decide to remove them. We had a few foxgloves completely eaten by caterpillars this summer, but I chose to leave them because I prefer to lose a couple of prolific self seeders like foxgloves and gain the beauty of the butterflies that eventually emerged.

We also suffered a real mould problem in the entire garden this year (due to the weather conditions apparently). We chose to dig out and destroy an entire flower bed rather than spray the whole garden with fungicide.

Only you can make the call as to what you choose to do.

Aphids

These little blighters love our roses. A reasonable amount of control can be had by blasting them with a strong jet of water from a hose or failing that a spritzer bottle of water mixed with a little washing up liquid can be effective.

Caterpillars

These transforming little critters can do a lot of damage. If you want to remove them, pick them off and dispose of them as you see fit. Wear gloves as some of them can irritate your skin. You can also plant flowering herbs such as dill or sweet woodruff to encourage natural enemies such as parasitic wasps which find caterpillars a tasty snack. Or use your own natural pesticide.

Leaf miners

These create pretty white patterns on the leaves of your plants. If you want to get rid of them pick off the affected leaves and destroy them, but you will be killing the little miner worms too.

Slugs and snails

We suffer a lot with snails as our garden is walled and they just love to live on the damp brick. I will confess my husband likes to teach the snails to fly through the air ... ahem. If you have a lot of time on your hands and infinite patience you can go out in the dark of night and hand pick off all the snails. You can also now purchase non-toxic slug pellets. Don't use chemical slug pellets if you have small children or pets. Remember that hedgehogs and birds also like to eat snails and if you have used chemical slug pellets the poison can be passed on. Slug beer traps are often very effective and make for very tipsy snails.

Slug beer trap

Sink a small pot into the soil beside vulnerable plants; put a little beer in the bottom. The snails smell the beer and fall in, but presumably by the time you find them the next morning they don't have a lot of cares left. You will need to empty the pot and refill regularly.

Diseases often attack with no warning and there is nothing you could have done to prevent them. However, keep your garden tools clean especially secateurs so that you don't inadvertently transfer disease. Examine plants regularly and act quickly if you do spot a problem. Remove infected leaves and burn them. Don't allow infected leaves to fall and sit on the soil and don't put them in the compost.

Bacterial disease can often be treated using a homemade garlic spray (see homemade pesticide).

Fungus can often be prevented from taking hold by using an alkaline solution.

Viruses are annoying but usually not fatal. These can cause curled leaves or spots. Remove and burn the affected leaves.

Natural homemade insecticides

Homemade insecticides have got to be better for your garden, the soil and the environment but remember they are basically a 'killer for insects' so they may have a toxic effect on other animals, humans and your soil. Choose the most effective one for you but bear in mind the harm it may cause to you and your area.

Oil spray – used for aphids and mites

Mix one cup of vegetable oil with one tablespoon of liquid soap and mix. When you need the spray add two teaspoons of the oil/ soap mix to two pints (1 litre) of water and shake well. Spray onto the plant surfaces.

Soap spray – use for aphids, mites, whitefly and beetles

Mix one and a half teaspoons of liquid soap with two pints (1 litre) of water. Spray onto the infected plants.

Garlic spray

Peel a head of garlic and blitz it in a blender with two cups of water. Strain, then use the liquid to spray on your plants.

Chilli spray – Use on a variety of pests

Mix one tablespoon of chilli powder with two pints (1 litre) of water and a few drops of liquid soap.

Or ... Blend half a cup of fresh chilli peppers with one cup of water and then add two pints of water and bring to the boil. Steep until cool then strain out the chilli pulp. Add a few drops of liquid soap and spray onto affected areas of the plant.

Multi-purpose spray

Blitz one bulb of garlic, one small onion and one teaspoon of cayenne pepper together and allow it to sit for an hour or so. Strain, then add one tablespoon of liquid soap and mix. Spray onto the tops and undersides of affected leaves. This mix will keep in the fridge for about a week.

Salt spray – for use on spider mites

Mix two tablespoons of sea salt with one gallon of warm water and spray on the affected areas of the plant.

Citrus soap spray – for slugs, ants and cockroaches

Mix three tablespoons of liquid soap with one ounce of orange essential oil and add to one gallon of water, mix well.

Natural homemade fungicides

Alkaline fungicide – Mix one heaped teaspoon bicarbonate of

soda with one tablespoon dormant oil (available from garden centres), half a teaspoon washing up liquid and four litres (1 gallon) of warm water. Dormant oil is typically a petroleum based oil but can sometimes be found as a vegetable based one. Soy bean oil can be used instead but I would add in a little garlic as well.

Baking soda fungicide

Mix one heaped tablespoon of baking soda with one gallon of water.

Apple cider vinegar fungicide

Mix two tablespoons of apple cider vinegar with one gallon of water.

Companion planting

Companion planting is a method of maintaining a natural balance in your garden and helps to keep pests away. It also provides help for pollination. This works because the companion plants usually have a strong scent that confuses pests and keeps them from their intended target (unless you have incredibly intelligent pests). Other companion plants will help attract beneficial insects such as lacewings and lady birds/bugs that like to feast on aphids.

Basil – repels mosquitoes but apparently also improves the flavour of most crops that grow near it.

Borage – the pollinators love the flowers, plant by tomatoes to deter pests.

Calendula/marigolds – plant by tomatoes to keep the whitefly away and beside beans to deter aphids. The ladybirds/bugs and hoverflies also love it as do the pollinators.

Catnip – repels flea beetles.

Chives – plant by chrysanthemums to deter aphids.

Fennel – the flowers attract hoverflies that love to munch on aphids.

Garlic chive (Allium tuberosum) – plant with carrots to deter carrot root fly and by roses to deter aphids and possibly vampires.

Lavender – apart from attracting bees, butterflies and hoverflies it can be planted by carrots and leeks to confuse the pests.

Mint – plant mint next to carrots, tomatoes, alliums and brassicas. Keep the mint in a pot because it is a thug and if allowed free reign it will take over.

Nasturtiums – plant by runner and French beans and brassicas to entice the aphids away. The beneficial insects also love the flowers.

Sage – plant by your brassicas to attract bees and hoverflies but the scent also confuses pests.

Spring onions/scallions – plant among your carrots to deter carrot root fly and onion fly.

Thyme – keeps blackfly away if planted next to roses.

Wormwood – the flowers attract lacewings, ladybirds/bugs and hoverflies. The strong scent also keeps aphids at bay.

Tips: Try to avoid growing lots of the same plant in one spot, it can provide a super easy lunch table for pests or diseases.

Herbs placed throughout the garden provide scent that may deter pests from your prize flowers.

Note: Some plants make bad neighbours to each other; avoid causing a plant punch up.

Garlic and onions are good neighbours for most but don't plant near beans or peas as their growth can be impaired.

Potatoes don't get on with sunflowers.

Cabbage and cauliflower do not like each other.

Plant feed tea

We are used to hearing the term herbal tea and you may have drunk a cup of two. But what about herbal tea for your plants? It can be used to water your plants and add nutrients from the herbal blend.

You don't even need to boil the kettle! Most plant teas are made by soaking your chosen herbs for a few days in a bucket of water. Stir it occasionally to help release all the goodness. The choice of herbs will depend on what you have. You can use a single herb or create a blend.

Some suggestions:

Alfalfa, comfrey, dill, couch grass, coltsfoot, nettle, dandelion, yarrow, horsetail, sunflower, fenugreek, mint, hops, raspberry leaves, coneflower, soapwort, sage, garlic.

A general rule of thumb is five ounces of dried herb to 6 gallons of water. Pop your herbs or herb blend into an old pillowcase and plunge it into the bucket of water. Mix it every day and leave for at least five days. Then wring out the water from the herb bag. Fresh herbs can be used but you will need about three times as much compared to the dried. Use to water your plants and don't waste the squidgy herbs, they can be spread as a compost or added to your compost heap.

Gardening by the moon

A lot of gardeners, even those that aren't witches, plant and harvest by the phases of the moon. You can still find almanacs that list what to plant and when in line with astrological timings. Think how much the moon affects the sea and her tides, so it must affect the earth and how things grow too. It might initially sound confusing but once you get the hang of it, the results will be rewarding.

A waxing moon is good for planting.

Fruit for eating straight away should be picked on a waxing moon.

A waning moon is good for planting plants that fruit below ground such as potatoes.

A waning moon is good for pruning, weeding and harvesting food to be stored.

Just after a new moon, plant leafy vegetables and herb seeds.

Waxing moon – pot cuttings, re-pot house plants; pick herbs, fruit and vegetables for eating straight away.

On a full moon, plant vegetables such as tomatoes, peppers and onions (any type of 'watery' vegetables and fruit). Fertilise your plants on a full moon too.

Just after a full moon, plant tuber vegetables such as carrots and potatoes, also biennials and perennials.

On a waning moon, start a compost heap, weed, cut and prune, pick fruits and flowers, herbs and vegetables that will be stored.

Close to the dark moon, cut timber and spray any fruit trees (preferably with eco-friendly spray).

And then you have the categories for the astrological signs. Here is a list of each type of energy, either barren, productive, semi fruitful or fruitful:

Moon in Aries – Barren
Moon in Taurus – Productive
Moon in Gemini – Barren
Moon in Cancer – Fruitful
Moon in Leo – Barren
Moon in Virgo – Barren
Moon in Libra – Semi-fruitful
Moon in Scorpio – Fruitful
Moon in Sagittarius – Barren
Moon in Capricorn – Productive
Moon in Aquarius – Barren
Moon in Pisces – Fruitful

Another useful guide is:

Above soil level plants – these are the plants that will produce crops above the ground; these should be sown the day after the new moon up until the first quarter, preferably in a fertile or semi-fertile astrological sign.

Annuals – plant the day after the new moon up until the day before the first quarter, preferably in a fertile or semi-fertile astrological sign.

Below soil level plants – these are the plants that crop under the ground. These should be planted during the day after the full moon, preferably in a fertile or semi-fertile astrological sign.

Biennials and perennials – this category includes shrubs and trees. Begin planting the day after the full moon and up to the day before the last quarter preferably in a fertile or semi-fertile astrological sign.

Seed collection – this is best done at the full moon when the moon is in a fire or air astrological sign such as Aries, Leo, Sagittarius, Libra, Gemini or Aquarius.

Harvesting – Fruit and vegetables are best harvested during

the waning moon and when the moon is in a barren or semi-barren fire or air sign such as Aries, Leo, Sagittarius, Libra, Gemini or Aquarius.

Zones

You will need to be aware of the zone you live in to work out which plants you can and cannot grow due to hardiness i.e. whether they will survive lower temperatures. The zones have been worked out based on the minimum ten-year winter temperatures. The zone maps were first developed by the Department of Agriculture in the USA but have now been applied to most of the globe. Bear in mind that these zones are only guidelines, Mother Nature doesn't always play by the rules.

I have included maps for the UK and USA for reference. The UK lies somewhere between the zones 6 and 9 based on the USA guidelines.

Plant Hardiness:

USDA Zone	Temperature Celsius	Temperature Fahrenheit
0a	<53.9	-65
0b	-53.9 to-51.1	-65 to-60
1a	-51.1 to-48.3	-60 to-55
1b	-48.3 to-45.6	-55 to-50
2a	-45.6 to-42.8	-50 to-45
2b	-42.8 to-40	-45 to-40
3a	-40 to-37.2	-40 to -35
3b	-37.2 to-34.4	-35 to-30
4a	-34.4 to-31.7	-30 to-25
4b	-31.7 to-28.9	-25 to-20
5a	-28.9 to-26.1	-20 to-15
5b	-26.1 to-23.3	-15 to-10
6a	-23.3 to-20.6	-10 to-5
6b	-20.6 to-17.8	-5 to 0
7a	-17.8 to-15	0 to 5
7b	-15 to-12.2	5 to 10
8a	-12.2 to-9.4	10 to 15
8b	-9.4 to-6.7	15 to 20
9a	-6.7 to-3.9	20 to 25
9b	-3.9 to-1.1	25 to 30
10a	-1.1 to 1.7	30 to 35
10b	1.7 to 4.4	35 to 40
11a	4.4 to 7.2	40 to 45
11b	7.2 to 10	45 to 50

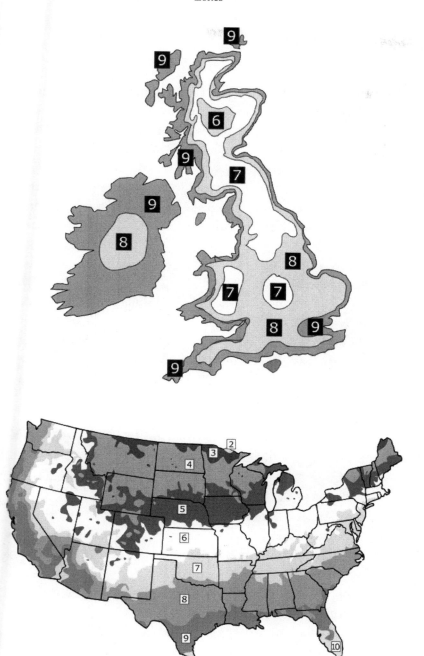

Floromancy and botanomancy

Divination with natural objects such as flowers and plants can be an interesting project to delve into.

Botanomancy is divination using plants and floromancy is divination using flowers.

Once you get to know your garden you will begin to understand what is usual and what isn't. Differences in how a plant looks and grows or how the wildlife acts can be taken as a sign or message. But you can also use plant items specifically for divination.

Stems from tall plants such as yarrow or chives can be used in a system like iChing.

Flowers, herbs and seed heads can be floated on the surface of water for scrying.

Herbs and leaves can be burnt to read the smoke for messages.

Pop some bay leaves onto charcoal or an open fire and visualise your question. If the leaves burn with a bright flame and crackle loudly then the answer is positive, if they fizzle out and smoulder, sadly then the answer is no.

Create a divination set using dried seed and flower heads to cast as you would with runes.

Press flowers and leaves and stick them to card to create your own oracle deck.

Vervain, fig and sycamore leaves are particular favourites for using in Botanomancy. Plants that have showy flowers, spikes or thorns are especially good. Plants can be thrown on the fire and then the smoke or the ashes are read. Sometimes a question or symbols to represent a question are carved on the branches before burning them.

Words written on leaves especially those of the fig and sage can be released to the wind. The leaves that are not blown away reveal the answer to a question.

Folklore has its fair share of flower and plant divination:
When spring finally arrives the first flower that appears in your garden has a meaning, depending on what day of the week it arrives.

Monday – brings good fortune.
Tuesday – assures success in your ventures.
Wednesday – brings marriage or a partnership.
Thursday – a bit of caution and vigilance are required going
    forward.
Friday – immense wealth is coming your way.
Saturday – ruh roh ... bad luck.
Sunday – good luck will follow you.

So perhaps in the first few days of spring don't go outside on a Saturday ...

And of course, there is the classic 'love me, love me not' chant said whilst pulling petals from a daisy. This can be used with any flowers to gain a positive or negative answer.

If you want to dream of your true love, place a bay or holly leaf under your pillow.

Korean ladies would place three carnations in their hair to see which one died first. If it was the top one then it would mean her later years of life would be hard, the middle one meant her younger years would be difficult and if the bottom one died first she was doomed to a life of hard work and disappointments. Seriously, I just wouldn't put the flowers there in the first place!

The Victorians believed that if you placed two flower buds in a vase, each one with the initials of a couple attached to it you would find out where the relationship was headed. The vase would be hidden away for a week or so then taken out so that the flowers could be examined. The state of the blooms and whether the stems or flowers were touching would indicate whether a marriage was imminent or not.

Plant dyes and inks

Roots, nuts and flowers can provide you with natural dyes. Collect flowers in full bloom and make sure any nuts or berries you use are ripe. Experiment with different plant materials to create a variety of colours.

As a general guide:

Chop the plant material and add to a pan.

Cover with double the quantity of water and bring to the boil, simmer for one hour.

Strain out the plant material – now you have your plant dye liquid.

To set the colour on the fabric you may have to soak the fabric in a colour fixative, called a mordant, before dying.

Mordant:

Berry dyes: ½ cup salt to eight cups cold water.

Plant dyes: One-part vinegar to four parts cold water.

Put the fabric in the fixative and simmer in a pan for an hour. Rinse until clear then squeeze out the excess water.

Place the wet fabric in a pan containing the plant dye liquid. Simmer until you get the desired colour.

Alternatively place the wet fabric in a bowl with the plant dye liquid and leave to soak overnight.

When washing home-dyed fabric after colouring, wash separately as the dye may leech out.

Here are some suggested plants and a rough guide on their colour:

Orange: Alder bark, bloodroot roots, carrots, eucalyptus

leaves and bark, giant coreopsis, onion skin, pomegranate skin, St John's wort flowers, turmeric.

Pink: Bloodroot roots, avocado skin and seed, cherries.

Yellow: Eucalyptus leaves and bark, broom bark, ivy twigs, crab apple bark, agrimony, yarrow, bay, broom flowers, chamomile flowers, fenugreek, goldenrod leaves, plantain.

Green: Eucalyptus leaves and bark, pomegranate skin, dock leaves, agrimony, angelica, artichoke, broom stem, chamomile leaves, grass, marjoram, nettles, mint, sage, sorrel roots, yarrow.

Brown: Eucalyptus leaves and bark, onion skin, boiled acorns, beetroot, birch bark, broom bark, burdock, coffee grounds, dandelion roots, fennel flowers and leaves, hops, ivy twigs, juniper berries, oak bark, dried oregano stems, pine bark.

Red: St John's wort flowers, burdock, comfrey, crab apple bark, dandelion root, dock leaves, dried hibiscus flowers, sycamore bark, dark hollyhock petals.

Burgundy/purple: Beetroot, blackberries, blueberries, red cabbage, basil, dark hollyhock petals.

Blue: Cornflower petals, dogwood bark, elderberry, red cabbage, purple iris, fresh woad leaves.

Grey/black: Alder, iris roots, meadowsweet, oak galls, basil.

Plant Ink

It can be fun to make ink from plants. The ink can then be used in magical workings, especially if you correspond the colour and the plant used in the ink to the intent of the spell. I like to use it to write out petitions. A general guide:

One cup fresh or half a cup of dried plant material,
One cup of water,
One cup of mordant, if necessary (see recipe in the plant dye chapter),

Half a teaspoon gum Arabic.

Simmer water, plant material and mordant for half an hour, then strain.

Mix in half a teaspoon of gum Arabic while the liquid is still warm and allow to cool.

This will make about three to four ounces of ink.

Some plant materials don't need a mordant to fix them such as tea, turmeric or onion. Others need the mordant to keep the colour.

You can also add a mordant by dropping a piece of rusty iron into the pot with the water and plant material or use sodium carbonate if you don't want to use the mordant recipe.

Gum Arabic helps to make the ink smoother and thicker whilst also preserving the colour and helping the ink flow.

Adding three drops of thyme essential oil to your finished ink will also help to prevent mould forming.

Experiment with different plant materials to create colours and see what works best for you. (Use the plant colour chart from the plant dye chapter.)

Trees

Trees can create a focal point and a significant impact on your garden design. They also have their own unique magical properties. Each one will have a dryad or spirit within. I encourage you to connect with any of the trees on your land (or elsewhere). To connect with the dryad of a tree is very special. Always approach a tree with respect and ask if you can connect with the spirit first. Some trees may not want direct contact, listen to their wishes.

You can use the leaves, flowers and seeds from trees in magical workings but also fallen twigs. If you want to make something larger such as a wand that requires you to cut a piece from the tree, always ask permission first. And take great care to make a clean cut and not damage the rest of the tree. Remember to leave an offering in thanks.

I am of the opinion that if you are meant to make a wand or a staff, the tree will drop the wood for you to use without the need for you to cut anything from the tree, but follow your own intuition.

Trees also offer good meditation spots – to sit under the branches and lean up against the trunk but also provide a good spot to leave offerings; not only to the tree dryads but also to deity and the fae. There is a practice of tying ribbons to tree branches to make blessings and wishes. This is a lovely idea but please be mindful to only use biodegradable materials and to tie any bindings loosely to allow the tree to grow uninhibited.

This is a basic list of tree properties but each one will have an individual personality. Get to know it and find out what wisdom and magic it can share with you:

Apple – Love, healing, clarity, knowledge, abundance and spirit work.

Apricot – Peace, love, passion and romance.

Ash – Protection, prosperity, dispels negativity, health, dreams, love, intuition, sea magic, luck, hex breaking and courage.

Avocado – Beauty, passion, love and fertility.

Banana – Prosperity and spirituality.

Beech – Wishes, creativity, spirituality, divination, luck and success.

Birch – Purification, protection, exorcism, new beginnings, courage, fertility, love and release.

Blackthorn – Protection, exorcism, divination and healing.

Brazil nut – Love and prosperity.

Cashew – Prosperity and energy.

Cedar – Purification, money, protection and goddess work.

Cherry – Love, fertility, divination and beginnings.

Chestnut – Love, strength, success, prosperity, abundarce and fertility.

Date – Spirituality, death and rebirth and offerings.

Elder – Purification, healing, fairy work, protection, intuition, exorcism, hex breaking and rebirth.

Elm – Love, balance, luck, energy and psychic abilities.

Eucalyptus – Moon magic, sun magic, divination, dreams, healing and purification.

Fig – Meditation, love, fertility and divination.

Hawthorn – Happiness, fertility, love, protection, purification, forgiveness, fairy work and hope.

Hazel – Fertility, wishes, love, protection, luck, wisdom, divination, healing, inspiration and prosperity.

Holly – Protection, luck, dreams, balance and success.

Lemon – Purification, moon magic, happiness, decisions, uplifting, love, protection, friendship and fidelity.

Lime – Purification, love, healing, protection and energy.

Macadamia – Prosperity.

Maple – Love, money, attraction, positive energy, healing and binding.

Nutmeg – Money, luck, fidelity and protection.

Oak – Healing, health, protection, money, fertility, luck, strength, vitality and power.

Orange – Love, happiness, uplifting and generosity.

Peach – Love, fertility, spirituality, wishes and longevity.

Pear – Passion, love, prosperity and luck.

Pine – Centring, focus, dragon magic, protection, truth, abundance, purification, fertility and healing.

Plum – Love, spirituality, relaxation, passion, longevity, wisdom and rebirth.

Purification – Clarity, energy and fidelity.

Rowan – Psychic abilities, power, success, protection, love, spirituality, fairy work, divination, healing and inspiration.

Sandalwood (red) – Meditation and love.

Sandalwood (white) – Death rites, purification, wishes and psychic abilities.

Walnut – Wishes, mental powers, clarity and fertility.

Willow – Love, protection, healing, cleansing, wishes, release, inspiration and intuition.

Witch hazel – Protection, divining, balance and grief.

Yew – Death and rebirth, transformation, astral travel, ancestors and knowledge.

The magic of flowers and flower language

There are also flowers associated with each month, which can be used in your magical workings. Whether you use the correspondence to tie in with the date you are working the spell or the month of birth for the person you are working the spell for, it will add power to it. There are various lists around but here is a suggestion:

> January – carnations, snowdrops
> February – iris, violets, primrose
> March – daffodil
> April – daisy, sweet pea
> May – lily of the valley, hawthorn
> June – rose, honeysuckle
> July – larkspur/delphinium, waterlily
> August – gladioli, poppy
> September – aster, morning glory
> October – marigold, calendula, cosmos
> November – chrysanthemum
> December – poinsettia, narcissus

Victorian flower language

Although flowers have had 'meanings' for centuries, it was the Victorians that really jumped on the bandwagon with this idea. The flower that was given to you by a friend or intended had its very own message – forget me not would mean 'true love', daisy would mean 'innocence' and thistle would mean 'I will never forget thee'. Although I am not sure about some of the messages personally, such as sage that meant 'domestic virtues' and daffodil that meant 'delusive hope'. The list is huge and varied but the following will give you some idea:

Apple blossom – good fortune

Aster – love

Azalea – passion, take care

Bachelor's Buttons – celibacy

Balm – sympathy

Begonia – beware

Bittersweet – truth

Bluebell – gratitude, humility

Broom – humility

Buttercup – riches, childlike

Camellia (pink) – longing

Camellia (white) – adoration, perfect

Camellia (red) – passion

Carnation (pink) – never forget you

Carnation (red) – my heart longs for you

Carnation (white) – innocence, pure love

Carnation (yellow) – disappointment

Celandine – joy

Chickweed – holding on to you

Chrysanthemum – abundance

Chrysanthemum (white) – truth

Chrysanthemum (red) – love

Cornflower – refinement

Cowslip – healing, youth, grace

Crocus – cheer, gladness

Cyclamen – goodbye

Daffodil – respect, unrequited love

Dahlia – dignity, elegance, forever yours

Daisy – innocence, loyalty, pure, beauty

Dandelion – faithful, happiness

Delphinium – fun

Dill – lust

Edelweiss – courage

Elderflower – zeal

Euphorbia – persistence

Forget me not – true love, memories

Forsythia – anticipation

Foxglove – youth

Freesia – trust, innocence

Fuchsia – love

Gardenia – secret love, purity

Geranium – friendship

Gerbera – innocence

Gladioli – generosity

Goldenrod – be cautious, encouragement

Harebell – humility, grief

Heather – admiration, wishes

Heliotrope – devotion

Hibiscus – consumed by love

Holly – defence, forgotten

Hollyhock – fruitfulness

Honesty – sincerity

Honeysuckled – love

Hyacinth – consistency, sorry

Hydrangea – understanding

Iris – faith, promise, hope

Ivy – affection

Jasmine – sensuality, grace

Larkspur – open heart

Lavender – love, devotion

Lilac – beauty, pride, emotions

Lily (white) – purity

Lily (yellow) – false, gratitude

Lily of the valley – sweetness, happiness

Magnolia – nobility

Mallow – beauty, sweetness

Marigold – love, affection, sorrow

Marjoram – happiness

Mint – virtue

Mistletoe – affection, kisses

Morning glory – affection

Motherwort – secret love

Mugwort – tranquillity

Mullein – good nature

Myrtle – love, joy

Nasturtium – conquest

Oak – bravery

Orchid – love, beauty

Pansy – you are in my thoughts

Parsley – knowledge

Peach blossom – I am captivated

Peony – shame, happy marriage, compassion

Periwinkle – memories

Petunia – I am soothed by you

Poppy (red) – pleasure

Poppy (white) – consolation

Poppy (yellow) – success

Primrose – I can't live without you

Rhododendron – danger

Rose (pink) – happiness, secret love, indecision

Rose (red) – love

Rose (white) – innocence, silence

Rose (yellow) – joy, jealousy

Rosemary – remembrance

Sage – wisdom, respect

Snapdragon – gracious, strength

Snowdrop – hope, consolation

Sunflower – adoration

Sweet pea – thank you but goodbye

Tulip – perfect

Tulip (red) – believe me

Tulip (yellow) – your smile is sunshine

Valerian – accommodating
Verbena – sensibility
Vervain – enchantment
Violet – modesty, affection, virtue
Wormwood – do not be discouraged
Yarrow – heartache cure

Garden spells, blessings and ritual

You can work magic for all of your plants by charging the water, soil and plant feed with energy. Visualise positive light flowing into it before you use it and perhaps devise some chants to use. Create a chant to say each time you water to bring nourishing energy and growth, and one to use when you plant seeds or seedlings to encourage strong growth.

Tree blessing spell

When you plant a tree you could perform a small blessing ritual. Devise a chant and charge the water and soil before you put it in the ground. Maybe even pop a circle of pebbles or shells around the base of the trunk as an offering and blessing to promote strong and healthy growth.

Garden blessing spell

Sprinkle apple juice around your garden in a clockwise direction. Chant to bring blessings of love, peace and abundance.

Basil banishing spell

Draw a symbol on a basil leaf to represent what you want to be rid of. Leave the leaf out in the sun to dry. When it is done, burn the leaf to release the energy.

Courage spell

Wear a carnation in your hair or on your lapel to bring courageous energy.

Happiness spell

Plant cyclamen to bring happiness and joy to your garden and household. They also help with relationships and va va voom.

Fairy protection spell

Plant African violets or have them in your house to protect against fairy mischief, they will also help with spiritual energy and connection.

Money spell

Sprinkle money with dried chamomile or a chamomile solution to ensure money keeps coming in.

Bamboo brings prosperity energy with it, add a green crystal to the roots when planting it and money will come your way.

Sun energy

Bring daisies into the house or carry a dried daisy flower with you to draw upon the solar energy.

Protection

Red geraniums are often grown to bring protection to a witch's house. Having geraniums inside your house will encourage a hospitable atmosphere.

Anti-abuse spell

Carry a piece of lavender with you to help protect against verbal and emotional abuse.

Anti-gossip spell

Make a fetish using a marigold flower and a bay leaf tied together to protect against gossip.

Memory charm

Take a whiff of rosemary to clear your mind and improve your memory. If you are taking an exam or test, take a piece of rosemary with you.

Protection spell

Cactus plants are by their very nature protective, that's what the spines are there for. Use them in the garden (if your climate allows) or place them indoors beside doors and windows to bring in protection.

Wisdom spell

Sprinkle dried sage into your shoes so that you 'walk with wisdom'.

Garden blessing

Once you have your garden space laid out it is a nice idea to bless and consecrate it, just as you would a circle before ritual.

Ask for a blessing for your garden from your matron/patron deity, the gods in general, Mother Earth/Father Sky, the angels or whoever you work with.

How you work the blessing is up to you. You might like to work a full ritual or just a blessing, go with what feels right for you.

A simple blessing uses water; you could tie this in with your garden theme by using moon, sun or rain water. Add in a little salt if you wish and then sprinkle the water around the boundaries of your garden. Work clockwise and ask for blessings from the divine or the elements to fill the garden with love and happiness. You could even chant as you go around.

A chant idea:
In this garden of mine,
Let love and happiness entwine.
Fill it with joy and love,
And grow with abundance from above.

Bring in the elements:
Element of earth I invite you in,

With growth and abundance,
To my garden begin.

Element of air I invite you in,
With gentle breeze and wisdom,
To my garden begin.

Element of fire I invite you in,
With passion and energy,
To my garden begin.

Element of water I invite you in,
With care and emotion,
To my garden begin.

My poetry is pretty bad, but you get the idea. It doesn't have to rhyme, sometimes the best chants and quarter calls are spontaneous, say what comes into your heart.

As you work with your garden through the seasons your energy will be added to it. As you care for it, planting, weeding, watering and pruning you will be putting positive energy in. But it doesn't hurt to re-bless the garden every so often. You could tie it in with each full or new moon, on the sabbats or at the beginning of each new season. Create a chant to use each time you water or when you feed the plants to help them prosper and grow.

Blessings of the Elements Ritual

This ritual was co-written by our lovely Kitchen Witch Coven ritual squad, so with thanks to Sue Perryman, Vanessa Armstrong, Joshua Petchey, Gwyneth Sangster and Tracey Roberts for allowing me to use it here.

The original was written for a group ritual, but I have adapted it here for a solitary, so that you can perform it in your garden. You will need to do a little bit of preparation for this. You will need:

Bubbles

Incense and lighter

A dish of salt or soil

A dish of water

Spray bottle filled with water and a few drops of lavender essence (or an air essential oil of your choice, or lavender flowers)

A small pouch/bag

A pebble

A shell

A match

A feather

A drink and cake

Work out which direction is North in your garden. Place the pebble on the ground in the North. Put the feather and the lavender water in the East, and the match in the South and the dish of water and shell in the West. Place the other items in the centre in front of you.

Casting the circle: Walk the circle four times. If your garden is small you can just turn around in a circle on the spot in the centre of your garden.

Once blowing soap bubbles (air).

Once with incense (fire) then place the incense in the South.

Once sprinkling salt or soil (earth) and place the salt/soil dish in the North, you may want to avoid sprinkling the salt on the garden earth.

Once sprinkling water (water).

Circle casting chant:
By the elements of four,
Cast this circle sky to floor.
Element of earth, rock and soil,
Element of air, breath and wind,

Element of fire, energy and passion,
Element of water, intuition and emotion.
By the elements of four,
Cast this circle sky to floor,
Energy within, energy without,
This blessings of the elements circle is now cast.

Quarters called:
Guardian of the North, element of Earth.
You are the foundation and mother of all things.
You provide stability, wisdom, knowledge, strength and growth.
As I press my hands on your fresh soil, may I connect with your
    energies.
I call on you to watch over my ritual today.
Welcome!

Guardian of the East, element of Air,
Through our breath we are connected.
And through our thoughts we have ideas, beliefs and inspiration,
We thank you for the dawn of each new day, bringing us limitless
    possibilities and infinite potential.
I call on you to watch over me during my ritual.
Welcome!

Guardian of the South, element of fire, I invite thee.
Bringer of destruction, giver of new life.
Your high energy evokes passion and ambition in all we do.
You are the warmth that carries us through the coldest winters.
And the stars that light our darkest nights.
You are the transformation that helps us grow.
And the will power to shape our futures, the embodiment of
    spirituality.
Welcome!

Element of Water, Guardian of the West,

Through you we experience our flowing, mutable feelings of love, compassion and our psychic awareness.

You watch over our sacred wells and springs; our gentle streams yet bring us storms and raging seas.

Your duality of nature is destructive, yet we cannot sustain life without you.

I call upon you to be present and watch over me during my ritual and bid you, welcome!

Calling in deity:

I call upon Ceres, Goddess of the grain and fertile earth.

You have the power to feed our lands.

You give us the gift of harvest.

Teach us how to sow our seeds of life, to nurture ourselves and to grow strong,

So that we may reap a bountiful harvest.

Welcome!

I call upon Shu, the Egyptian God of air and the winds who gives the breath of life to all living creatures and protects the Sun god Ra as he makes his journey through the night sky.

He supports the heavens and separates his children, the sky Nut and the earth Geb.

Ancient one, I ask you to join me and lend me your protective energies. Welcome!

Goddess of Fire, spirit of dance, Pele, I invite thee.

You are the goddess of creation, destruction, volcanoes and lightning.

You reward the generous with warmth and life,

Punishing the greedy with death and devastation.

You gift us with catastrophe, so we may look inward, finding our hidden passions to follow our own true spiritual paths.

Welcome!

Tiamet, Goddess of the salt sea, primordial Goddess of creation, who, through your sacred marriage with the fresh water oceans, created the Cosmos.

Yours is the beauty of the feminine when depicted as the 'glistening one', keeper of our life-force, our blood, sweat and tears.

I invite you to be present and ask that you guard, guide and protect me today.

Welcome!

Element shapeshifting

Close your eyes and take a few deep breaths. Feel yourself becoming calm and relaxed with each out breath, letting go of all the worries of the day. Feel any tension leave your body as we prepare to shapeshift with the elements.

Turn to face North, the direction of the element of earth. Visualise, feel and sense the element – what does it mean to you? This could be a mountain, a dark cave, a forest of trees, or just the area in your garden dedicated to this element. Allow the images to fill your mind. What scents are conjured up? What sounds relate to this element? Breathe them all in, deep into your core. Allow yourself to be enveloped by this element. Stay with it for as long as you would like to then gradually let the energy of this element leave your body and flow into the ground.

Turn to face East, the direction of the element of air. Visualise, feel and sense the element – what does it mean to you? This could be standing on a windy mountain top, laying down watching the clouds float past, or just the area in your garden dedicated to this element. Allow the images to fill your mind. What scents are conjured up? What sounds relate to this element? Breathe them all in, deep into your core. Allow yourself to be enveloped by this element. Stay with it for as long as you would like to then gradually let the energy of this element leave your body and flow into the ground.

Turn to face South, the direction of the element of fire. Visualise, feel and sense the element – what does it mean to you? This could be a large bonfire, throwing herbs into a fire pit, watching a candle flame, or just the area in your garden dedicated to this element. Allow the images to fill your mind. What scents are conjured up? What sounds relate to this element? Breathe them all in, deep into your core. Allow yourself to be enveloped by this element. Stay with it for as long as you would like to then gradually let the energy of this element leave your body and flow into the ground.

Turn to face West, the direction of the element of water. Visualise, feel and sense the element – what does it mean to you? This could be standing on the beach in front of the ocean, floating in a boat down the river, standing in the rain, or just the area in your garden dedicated to this element.

Allow the images to fill your mind. What scents are conjured up? What sounds relate to this element? Breathe them all in, deep into your core. Allow yourself to be enveloped by this element. Stay with it for as long as you would like to then gradually let the energy of this element leave your body and flow into the ground.

Take a few deeper breaths now and when you are ready open your eyes. Welcome back to your garden and this reality.

Forming the Element blessing:

Walk through each element/direction, starting with Earth and then moving around the circle to the next one until you have been through all four. At each one pick up the item you have placed there and pop it in your pouch and perform the blessing.

Earth:

Pick up the pebble and put it in your pouch.

Sprinkle yourself with salt (or soil) and say:

I am blessed and honoured with the element of earth.

Air:

Pick up the feather and put it in your pouch.

Spray or sprinkle yourself with lavender water and say:

I am blessed and honoured with the element of air.

Fire:

Pick up the match and put it in your pouch.

Waft yourself with incense and say:

I am blessed and honoured with the element of fire.

Water:

Pick up the shell and put it in your pouch.

Sprinkle yourself with moon water and say:

I am blessed and honoured with the element of water.

When you are done stand in the centre of the circle and ask for blessings from spirit to charge your element pouch.

Next raise some energy with a continuous chant:

Earth my body, water my blood, air my breath and fire my spirit.

When you feel that enough energy has been raised send the energy out to the Universe, to someone you know that needs it for healing or to your garden to help it grow.

Feasting and drinking:

Now you can sit for a short while and ground by drinking a cuppa and eating some cake, whilst perusing your garden.

Thanking deity:

Great Goddess Tiamet, I acknowledge your presence here with me today and thank you for your life-giving energies that sustain all life on earth.

I thank you too for your guidance and protection and bid you thanks and farewell!

Goddess Pele, I thank you.
You have taught us to embrace the chaos of destruction in our lives,
to dig deep and find our inner passions, so we may transform like
fire to find a new fate.
   You remind us of the sensuality and heat of new love, And give
us strength to act on our desires.
   Thanks, and farewell!

Shu, God of air and the winds we thank you for your presence
   during our ritual.
For guiding and protecting me and for giving us the breath of life.
Thanks, and farewell!

Ceres, thank you for your presence in this circle today.
For showing us how to connect with the earth that we stand on.
And in turn, connecting with ourselves and each other.
To grow and to share our harvests.
Thanks, and farewell!

Closing the quarters:
Element of water, we thank you for your gifts, for the rain which
is needed to swell the grain and the spirals of life which are ever
changing.
   I bless your energies and thank you for your presence here today
and bid you thanks and farewell!

Guardian of the North, element of Earth,
I thank you for your presence here today,
For your fertile lands providing nourishment and life – the womb
   from which all things grow.
Your energies have provided us with wisdom, knowledge and
   grounding.

Thanks, and farewell!

Guardian of the East,
I thank you for watching over me during my ritual and for the
*   breath of life that connects us all.*
Stay if you will, go if you must.
Thanks and farewell.

Guardian of the South, element of fire, I thank you,
You have brought gifts of motivation and creativity.
Through your destruction we may adapt, grow and find new paths
*   to walk.*
You bring us the life, the will and the energy to achieve all we wish.
You purify this world of the old, so we may begin again,
Thanks, and farewell!

Closing the circle:
Walk the circle widdershins (anti clockwise) or stand on the spot
and turn:

By the elements of four I uncast this circle sky to floor.
Element of earth, rock and soil.
Element of air, breath and wind.
Element of fire, energy and passion.
Element of water, intuition and emotion.
By the elements of four.
Uncast this circle sky to floor.
Energy within, energy without.
This circle is now open but never broken.

Edible flowers and garden snacks

You may have guessed, but I like my food and finding that some of the flowers we grow in our garden for decorative purpose are actually edible is a total bonus. Please do make sure you identify the flower correctly before scoffing it, we don't want any accidents or worse.

Edible flowers can be added to salads, desserts, cordials, oils, dressings, butters, soups and cakes. Experiment and see how they work for you.

Pick young flowers and buds. Use them straight away, although most of them will keep well in a bag in the fridge for a couple of days. Generally, only the petals are eaten, some of the green bases of the flower heads can be a little bitter tasting.

If you are going to eat flowers I would recommend only eating those you have grown yourself so that you know they are pesticide free. Make sure you wash them well and remove any insects that might be hiding ...

Allium – the blossoms from all the allium family are edible – chives, garlic, leeks etc.

Alpine pinks (Dianthus) – has a faint clove flavour. Works well in sugars, oils and vinegars.

Angelica (A. archangelica) – for sweet dishes.

Basil flowers (Ocimum basilicum) – sweet tasting flowers for salads and oils.

Bergamot (Monardia didyma) – spicy flavour that works well in herbal tea and savoury dishes.

Borage (Borage officinalis) – these taste like cucumber and can be used in salads, cakes and desserts.

Chive flowers (Allium schoenoprasum) – use in salads, egg and fish dishes.

Chrysanthemum/calendula – both are good in savoury dishes.

Citrus – the blossoms from orange, lemons, limes and grapefruit are highly scented and bring that flavour to any dish.

Clover flowers (Trifolium pratense) – red or white can both be used in salads.

Cornflower/bachelors buttons (Centaurea cyanus) – a mild clove flavour for cakes, desserts and herbal teas.

Courgette (Zucchini) flowers – good in vegetable or cheese dishes they can also be stuffed with rice and deep fried in batter.

Daisy (Bellis perennis) – add to cakes and salads. Not a strong flavour, more for decoration.

Dandelion (Taraxacum officinale) – from the blossoms to the roots this plant can be eaten raw or cooked.

Dill flowers (Anethum graveolens) – an aniseed flavour for salads and savoury dishes.

Elderflower (Sambucus nigra) – make into wine or cordial. Dip the flower heads in batter and deep fry.

Fennel flowers (Foeniculum vulgare) – especially good in salads or fish dishes.

Hibiscus (Hibiscuc rosa sinensis) – a sweet citrus taste, add to herbal teas and desserts. Dried hibiscus flower heads look fabulous dropped into the bottom of champagne glasses.

Hollyhock (Alcea rosea) – remove all the pollen. Crystallise and use for decorating cakes and desserts.

Jasmine (Jasminum officinale) – use the flowers in tea.

Lavender (Lavendulan augustifolia) – works in all kinds of dishes from sweet through to savoury. Be careful with quantities as too much can make your dish taste of soap.

Lilac (Syringa vulgaris) – a floral taste, add to sweet dishes.

Mallow zebrina (Malva sylvestris) – a mild nutty flavour, use in desserts, cakes, salads and herbal teas.

Mint flowers (Mentha spp.) – excellent in sweet or savoury dishes.

Nasturtium (Tropaeolum majus) – a lovely peppery flavour for salads and pastas. Use the petals and the leaves.

Pansies (Viola tricolor) – use for decoration and garnishes.

Garden pea flowers (Pisum sativum) – flowers and young shoots are delicious in salads.

Peony (Paeonia lactiflora) – use the flowers in drinks and salads.

Polyanthus (Polyantus eliator) – for salads, desserts and cakes.

Pot marigold (Calendula officinalis) – a peppery taste for soups, vinegars, butters and cakes.

Primrose (Primula vulgaris) – beautiful fresh or crystallised on cakes and desserts.

Rose (Rosa) – flavour and decorate drinks, sugars, desserts and cakes.

Rosemary flowers (Rosmarinus officinalis) – for tomato dishes or to flavour oils and butters.

Runner bean flowers (Phaseolus coccineus) – the pretty red flowers can be added to lots of savoury dishes.

Scented geranium (Pelargonium) – the flowers are milder tasting than the leaves.

Sunflower (Helianthus annus) – use the petals in salads.

Sweet violet (Viola odorata) – for teas, desserts and cakes but also in savoury dishes.

Tiger lily (Lilium leucanthemum var. tigrinum) – use in salads, egg, fish and poultry dishes.

From the garden snacks

It wouldn't be one of my books without at least one or two recipes in would it? Even if you don't go in for the fruit and veg plot in your garden you can still grow a few herbs or even eat some of the edible flowers and add them to recipes.

Herbs and petals can be added to marinates, rubs, vinegars, butters, oils, salads, salsas, dressings, pesto, sauces, soups, risotto and even sweet custards and syrups.

Herbal oils

Flavoured oils are easy to make and also freeze well; they are a clever way of using up gluts of herbs.

Chop the herbs in a food processor and add enough olive oil to lightly coat the herbs (roughly three tablespoons of herbs to one tablespoon of oil). Divide into portions and freeze in bags.

Finely chopped herbs can also be frozen in your ice cube trays. Fill the tray with herbs and then pour over water to cover. Freeze until solid. Then you can pop them out of the tray and freeze in bags.

Herbal butters

These work well with softer herbs such as dill, parsley, thyme, basil, tarragon and marjoram. Wrapped in cling film, it will keep in the fridge for about a week and up to three months in the freezer.

Pulse 3 tablespoons (100g/3 ½ oz.) rinsed herb leaves into a blender or chop finely. Season to taste and then add 100g/3 ½ oz. butter. Pop in two teaspoons of lemon juice and whizz or beat until smooth.

Herb pesto

Use just one herb or a mixture of them such as basil, oregano and parsley. Mix together a total of eight tablespoons of herbs with two cloves of garlic, salt and pepper to taste and blitz roughly in a food processor or pound with a pestle and mortar. Blend until the mixture is mushy then add in 50g/1 ¾ oz. grated parmesan cheese and 100ml/3 ½ fl oz. olive oil. Mix to a thick paste. Use on pasta or add in a little vinegar to create a dressing.

Herb scones

Add two to three tablespoons of fresh chopped herbs into your usual scone mix. Parsley, sage, marjoram, thyme and rosemary all work well.

Herb cheese

Chop a few borage leaves, pick some blue borage flowers from the plant and pop them all into cottage or cream cheese. Season with salt and pepper and spread on bread or crackers. This also works well with soft herbs such as chives.

Lavender syrup

Put two teaspoons dried lavender flowers, 300g/10 oz. sugar and the zest of one lemon in a pan with 300ml/10 fl oz. water over a medium heat. Stir until the sugar has dissolved. Remove from the heat and allow to infuse for at least an hour, stirring occasionally. Put the pan over the heat again and bring to the boil without stirring. Turn up the heat and allow to bubble for about five minutes until the mixture thickens. Remove from the heat. Allow to cool a little then strain into a sterilised bottle. Cool completely then seal and store in a cool place. This will keep for up to six weeks.

Candied flowers

Remove the stalks. Beat an egg white until it is foamy. Dip each flower into the egg white then into some sugar. Place the flower on greaseproof paper and cover with another sheet of greaseproof paper. Pop into the oven on the lowest setting until dry. Store in an airtight container.

Flower sugar

Add flowers or herbs to a jar of sugar leaving a little space (don't fill the jar right to the top). Shake the jar each day for about two weeks, then sieve/pick out the flowers or herbs. Lavender, violets and thyme work well for this.

Nut butter

Roast 225/8 oz. nuts (hazelnuts, walnuts etc.) in the oven for about ten minutes on a medium heat and then blitz. Mix to a paste with 75g/3 oz. butter.

Chocolate nut spread

Add 110g/4oz melted dark, milk or white chocolate to the nut butter mix and you have chocolate spread.

Root coffee

If you want to avoid caffeine but need 'coffee' this makes an alternative. Note I didn't say 'good alternative', it is certainly something different to try.

Wash dandelion or chicory roots, dry then slice them and lay on a baking tray. Bake in a low oven (300F/150C/Gas2) until they are brown and snap easily. Grind them up and use as you would normal coffee.

Herb cookies

Butter 100g (3 ½ oz.)
Sugar 50g (1 ½ oz.)
Ground almonds 50g (1 ½ oz.)
Plain flour (all purpose) 100g (3 ½ oz.)
Tablespoon of herbs, chopped – this works well with basil, lemon balm and thyme but experiment and see what you like.

Preheat the oven to 180C/gas mark 4. Cream together the butter and sugar, add the ground almonds then the flour. Knead together on a lightly floured board to form a dough. Roll the dough in the chopped herbs until the leaves are amalgamated into the dough then roll it out into a 5cm diameter sausage. Slice into 1 cm thick slices.

Place the slices on a well-greased baking sheet lined with

non-stick baking parchment. Bake for 10-15 minutes until lightly golden. Remove at once and cool on a wire rack.

Lotions and potions for you

Rosemary water

Put one handful of rosemary (stalk and leaves) into a saucepan and add just enough cold water to cover the herbs. Bring tc the boil and simmer for five minutes. Allow to cool then strain. Rosemary water can be added to lotions and creams but also as a hair wash or to add to your bath.

Chamomile hair rinse

Pour 1 ½ pints/850ml of boiling water over one cup of chamomile flowers (dried or fresh) and leave to cool. Use as a floral rinse after washing your hair to bring out the natural shine (works best on blonde hair).

Herbal Salve

A basic salve recipe which you can add your own dried herbs to. Mix and match and see what works for you. I would advise looking up any unusual herbs to make sure they are not skin irritants. But the 'garden variety' herbs such as rosemary, comfrey, calendula, yarrow etc., work well.

2 cups oil such as olive, almond or jojoba
¼ cup beeswax pastilles
Approx. 5 tablespoons dried herbs/flowers

Infuse the herbs in the oil by either, popping them in an airtight jar and leaving for three to four weeks, shaking daily (the jar, not you) or you can heat the herbs in the oil over a VERY low heat in a double boiler for three hours, until the oil colours a nice green. Strain out the herbs through a cloth. Discard the herbs, keep the oil. Heat the infused oil in a double boiler with the wax until it has melted and combined. Pour into small jars.

Herbal Lotion

A lovely moisturising lotion which you can tailor to your own desire.

You will need ¾ cup olive, almond or jojoba oil
1/3 cup solidified coconut oil
2 tablespoons beeswax pellets
2 sprigs fresh rosemary, sage, mint or any other herb you
    want to use
2/3 cup distilled water
1/3 cup aloe vera gel

Using a double boiler over a very low heat, warm the oils, wax pellets and herbs until they are just melted. Remove the sprigs of herbs at this point and pour the mixture into a blender. Once it has cooled to room temperature mix together the water and aloe gel in a separate pot. Once your oil mixture has set, turn the blender on to a high speed and slowly pour the water and aloe mixture in. The lotion should become a light thick and creamy texture. Pour into clean jars.

Reference

If you are new to gardening or even if you are experienced and just need an answer to a query there are lots of places to get help.

Try your local library, they have huge resources of gardening books and let's face it they could do with our support, you don't want to lose your library. While you are in the library ask if there are any local gardening clubs.

Ask someone with experience, we probably all have a relative or friend that likes to garden or even a neighbour. They will be more than happy to talk about their gardens I am sure. My dad used to live in a cottage that had a low fence around the garden. People walking past would stop, lean over the fence and compliment him on the garden and ask questions all the time.

The internet has site upon site with help, advice and suggestions.

For plant help I like to use:

www.rhs.org.uk

www.garden.org

Beyond the garden gate

Working with plants, seeds and soil is a beautiful way of bringing you in touch with Mother Nature. It connects you with all the elements and gives you a direct line to a whole host of magical energy. It will not only provide a sanctuary for you to escape to but also a place to meditate, to work magic and to connect with the divine.

Create, design and experiment but most importantly make the garden yours.

MOON
BOOKS

Moon Books

PAGANISM & SHAMANISM

What is Paganism? A religion, a spirituality, an alternative belief system, nature worship? You can find support for all these definitions (and many more) in dictionaries, encyclopaedias, and text books of religion, but subscribe to any one and the truth will evade you. Above all Paganism is a creative pursuit, an encounter with reality, an exploration of meaning and an expression of the soul. Druids, Heathens, Wiccans and others, all contribute their insights and literary riches to the Pagan tradition. Moon Books invites you to begin or to deepen your own encounter, right here, right now.

If you have enjoyed this book, why not tell other readers by posting a review on your preferred book site. Recent bestsellers from Moon Books are:

Journey to the Dark Goddess
How to Return to Your Soul
Jane Meredith
Discover the powerful secrets of the Dark Goddess and transform your depression, grief and pain into healing and integration.
Paperback: 978-1-84694-677-6 ebook: 978-1-78099-223-5

Shamanic Reiki
Expanded Ways of Working with Universal Life Force Energy
Llyn Roberts, Robert Levy
Shamanism and Reiki are each powerful ways of healing; together,
their power multiplies. Shamanic Reiki introduces techniques to
help healers and Reiki practitioners tap ancient healing wisdom.
Paperback: 978-1-84694-037-8 ebook: 978-1-84694-650-9

Pagan Portals – The Awen Alone
Walking the Path of the Solitary Druid
Joanna van der Hoeven
An introductory guide for the solitary Druid, The Awen Alone
will accompany you as you explore, and seek out your own place
within the natural world.
Paperback: 978-1-78279-547-6 ebook: 978-1-78279-546-9

A Kitchen Witch's World of Magical Herbs & Plants
Rachel Patterson
A journey into the magical world of herbs and plants, filled with
magical uses, folklore, history and practical magic. By popular
writer, blogger and kitchen witch, Tansy Firedragon.
Paperback: 978-1-78279-621-3 ebook: 978-1-78279-620-6

Medicine for the Soul
The Complete Book of Shamanic Healing
Ross Heaven
All you will ever need to know about shamanic healing and how to
become your own shaman…
Paperback: 978-1-78099-419-2 ebook: 978-1-78099-420-8

Shapeshifting into Higher Consciousness
Heal and Transform Yourself and Our World with Ancient
Shamanic and Modern Methods
Llyn Roberts
Ancient and modern methods that you can use every day to
transform yourself and make a positive difference in the world.
Paperback: 978-1-84694-843-5 ebook: 978-1-84694-844-2

Readers of ebooks can buy or view any of these bestsellers by
clicking on the live link in the title. Most titles are published in
paperback and as an ebook. Paperbacks are available in traditional
bookshops. Both print and ebook formats are available online.

Find more titles and sign up to our readers' newsletter at
http://www.johnhuntpublishing.com/paganism
Follow us on Facebook at https://www.facebook.com/MoonBooks
and Twitter at https://twitter.com/MoonBooksJHP